CONTENTS

The mission of the Battenkill Conservancy is to preserve and enhance the
Battenkill watershed through conservation, education, advocacy and the
River Watch water quality program.

The Ondowa. The Battenkill. The Kill. Country of Rounded Hills. The Battenkill is a breathtaking river which has been central to economies of the towns and hamlets in the watershed, and is a numinous place of re-creation, where we make ourselves new again through the river's presence, through our presence in and near the Kill. The Battenkill is known by many people who are not from our region, primarily through artists and writers, and, of course, fly anglers. Like other famed trout streams in our region, the Battenkill is something of a Mecca destination for those of us who fly fish. What many may not pay attention to are streams and creeks that feed the river, places the locals know.

Yet it is easy to forget, or to fail to notice, that the Battenkill has a storied name beyond fishing, and that the farming communities and villages in and near the watershed declined and thrived, the river just doing what rivers always do, and that people who have lived their lives here have experiences that are intertwined with Washington County's landscape, with the twists and bends of the Kill.

Rivers are rivers, but they are also metaphoric. The river is a metaphor for time, always passing yet always remaining, always moving in a particular direction, but always present. This book, created through a partnership between the Battenkill Conservancy and Elizabeth and Barton Cockey, is as much about time as it is about the Battenkill, about people, our neighbors, for whom the Kill has been a strong part of their lives, if only in the background, but always in the background.

As varied as the people who live in the watershed, this anthology of memories, histories, pictures and art work, is rich in simple charm, untold stories and, of course, with pictures! How could anyone make a book about one of the world's most stunning rivers without pictures and art work? One needn't be an artist to find the Kill inspiring. As much about the Battenkill itself, this collection is about people who love the river, who work and live here. We know that rivers and humans are separable, but, in our fleeting lives, for a time at least, the Battenkill as recorded in this book reveals itself as a part of all of us who love the Kill. My belief is that our reverence for the river will be a guiding force that will help maintain its health and grandeur in perpetuity.

Yet it is generally the small, hardly noticed, simple things this book of the Battenkill celebrates. As it is only natural to have preferences, my favorite chapter is Winged Harbingers, about retired Cambridge science teacher Howard Romack's summer night discovery of a rare species of moth in his backyard. The story of its discovery is emblematic of the watershed, the Battenkill Valley, that where we live has rare, if not magical qualities. I think I might get a black light. Maybe they have one at the Salem Hardware. I'd like to see if I could lure and identify a Golden Ghost.

Dr. Stuart Bartow
Professor of English, SUNY Adirondack

The Rowboat
oil on canvas
looking at the bridge in Center Falls,
Greenwich, NY
Elizabeth Cockey
Collection of Mr. & Mrs. George Perkins

INTRODUCTION

This book is a collection of memories, lore and images of life in this most beautiful watershed of the Battenkill. Most of these stories will not be found anywhere else, not even in old newspapers. For instance, when we asked Sally Tefft, former owner of *The Greenwich Journal & Salem Press*, why nothing appeared in the paper at the time that toxic waste spilled from a local mill into the river (1969) she said she remembered the event, but that it must have happened on a Wednesday while the Journal was being printed. So it goes.

Human beings probably first saw the Battenkill as long as 12 thousand years ago, with the melting of the last glaciers. At that time, Stone Age migrants came through the river valleys. Among their descendants were the Iroquois, who called the river Ondawa, country of rounded hills. They hunted along her banks, fished, and traveled with canoes in the currents there, much as we do today.

Many of these stories are oral history accounts, as personal as they are unique, but all were told from the heart. This helped convey a greater depth of understanding that might otherwise only be told to a close friend; not to a passerby, and certainly not to a journalist looking for news. Several memorable events involve children, recalled by the very same people who have grown up, but described their memories as if the details had happened only yesterday.

The importance of the Battenkill as a valuable resource is especially significant as we look to the future. This is something that we feel is pertinent to all of us: families, communities, and the country as a whole. The necessity of having clean water and healthy farming practices, recreational use of the river, and a wild habitat for thousands of animal and plant species is vital as we go forward. Because the Battenkill flows on and on, still a mother to us all.

Elizabeth J. Cockey
October 2016

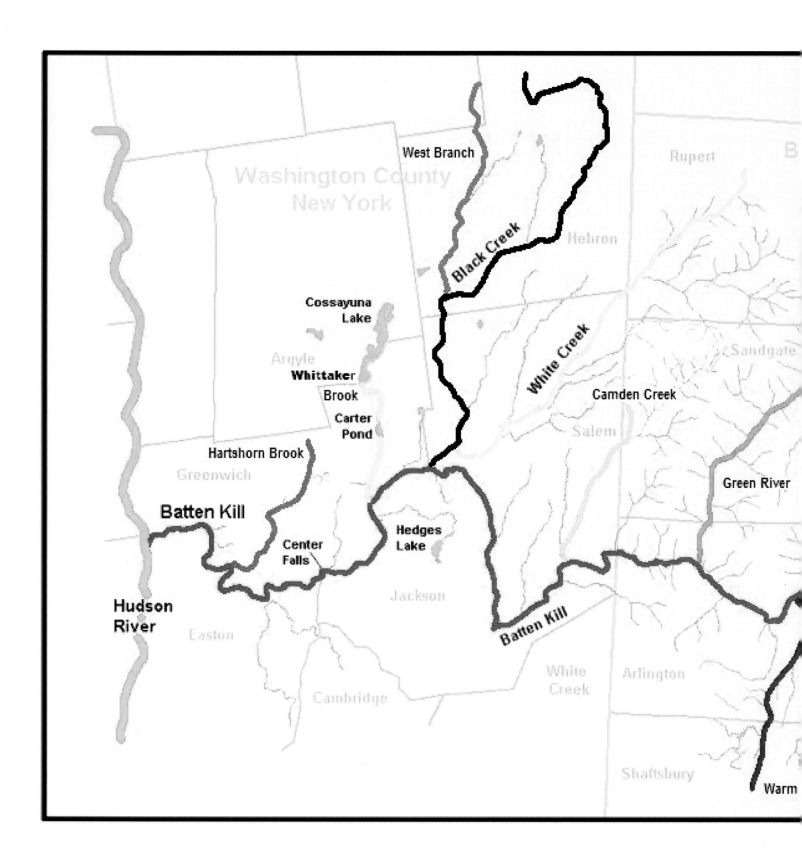

West Branch

Washington County New York

Black Creek

Rupert

Hebron

Cossayuna Lake

Argyle

White Creek

Sandgate

Whittaker

Camden Creek

Brook

Carter Pond

Salem

Hartshorn Brook

Greenwich

Green River

Batten Kill

Hedges Lake

Center Falls

Jackson

Hudson River

Easton

Batten Kill

White Creek

Arlington

Cambridge

Shaftsbury

Warm

1. HISTORY

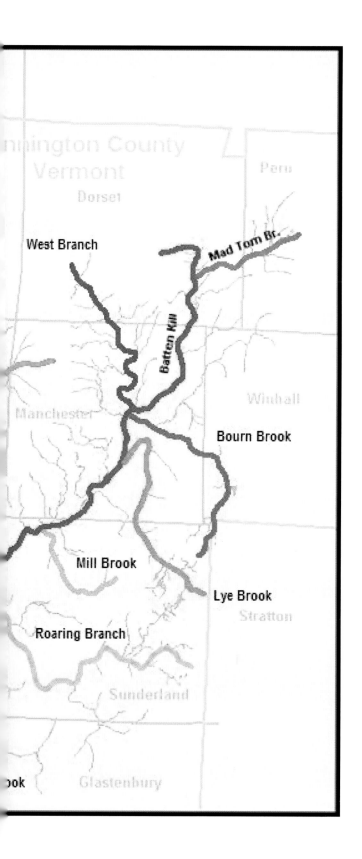

THE RIVER

The headwaters of the Battenkill seep out of the ground in the verdant hill country. A spongy meadow in East Dorset, Vermont feeds the uppermost end of the stream, but there are numerous tributaries in Vermont. In order of appearance as one proceeds downstream, the feeding branches within Vermont are called Mad Tom Branch, West Branch, Bourn Brook, Lye Brook, Mill Brook, Roaring Branch which merges with Warm Brook, and Green River. Smaller rivulets are too numerous to count, and the Vermont portion of the watershed comprises about 200 square miles. Camden Creek flows southward from its source in Vermont and joins the Battenkill on the New York side of the state line. The main tributary within New York is Black Creek, which receives the waters of White Creek and flows into the Kill a short distance west of Salem. Hartshorn Brook feeds in about half way between Center Falls and the Hudson. New York's portion of the watershed is about 207 square miles. Thus, the 59-mile-long river is about evenly shared between the two states. Even the winding main stream is pretty evenly split, with about 28 miles in Vermont.

The river flows down the Vermont Valley between the Green Mountains and the Taconics, but then it performs an unusual geological stunt, turning west at the level of Arlington to cut right through the Taconic range. You can view this part of the river from Route 313, which takes advantage of the same gap in the hills. In geological parlance, the Kill initially behaves as a "subsequent" stream, running parallel to the mountains, and suddenly changes into a "superimposed" stream, grinding its way across a mountain range. Because mountains do not spring up overnight, under some circumstances a strong river may continue to wear a groove through gradually uplifting terrain. But the Taconic mountain-building event was so incredibly long ago (550 to 440 million years) that the water courses of today are also a product of much more recent events, especially the relatively recent periods of glaciation which banked up sand and gravel in the Vermont Valley to the south of Arlington. The last glaciers covered northern New York with a sheet of ice a mile thick. When all that ice melted 12,000 to 10,000 years ago, the Battenkill must have been a torrent.(1)

The relatively calm river of today is a perfect place to admire the complex geology that created the lumpy hills that lend so much charm to the landscape. Tilted ridges of shale and slate traverse the stream, accumulating rocks behind them — and what an assortment of rocks! There is brilliant red slate transported from Granville by glaciers and floods. Dense boulders of red quartzite and chunks of green chlorite schist with snow-white quartz shine like gems through the clear water. Here and there on the shore, gnarled and twisted strata attest to the titanic collision of continental plates that thrust up the Taconic Mountains and eventually jammed all the lands of the earth together to create the supercontinent called Pangaea in a process that ended 300 million years ago. (As the reader will have noticed, the continents have since separated.)

Clues to this seemingly implausible story of continental drift first came from this very region. Ebenezer

Indian Artifacts - found on a farm near Greenwich, NY
Top L-R: Kirk Corner Notched, 9500-8500 B.P., Lamoka 5500-3500 B.P.
Mid L-R: Clovis, 15,000-1,000 B.P., stone beads, Wayland 3700-2700 B.P.
Bottom L-R: Madison, 1100-300 B.P., Levanne, 1300-600 B.P.
from the original collection of Fred Stevens

Emmons (1799-1863) was born in Massachusetts and studied at Williams College. He earned a medical degree but later pursued his real passion and studied geology, graduating from the Rensselaer School. Ever since childhood, he had hiked through the mountains, collecting rocks and fossils. He named the Adirondack Mountains and their principal peaks and named and studied the Taconic Mountains. (2) Based on his observations, he concluded that Lower Cambrian rocks lay on top of younger Ordovician rocks along what is now recognized as an overthrust that occurred during the collision of tectonic plates. In other words, the earth's crust cracked; and deeper, older rock slid upward and over the younger layers on the surface, like a slow-motion multi-car pile-up. His correct findings foreshadowed the modern

understanding of continental drift but put him at odds with the scientific consensus of the time. (3) When New York State Geologist James Hall responded with public ridicule and a lawsuit, Emmons compounded his woes by suing Hall for slander and libel. The courts ruled in Hall's favor, and Emmons emigrated to North Carolina, where he became the state geologist in 1852. There he continued to contribute to geological science, publishing extensive studies of the state's resources and providing the first description of the teeth of *Deinosuchus*, a giant, dinosaur-eating crocodile. Emmons died on his plantation in North Carolina, but his remains were eventually buried in Albany Rural Cemetery. In April of 1865, General Sherman's troops looted Emmons' office in the statehouse in Raleigh. Most of his

specimens and reports, "as well as 'sufficient manuscript to make 1200 octavo pages of published reports,' were lost or destroyed."(4)

The most spectacular waterfall is the seventy-five foot drop, just west of Middle Falls, known as *Dionondahowa*.

When the mighty continental collision forced up the mountains, they were far higher than the

eroded hills we see today, but the Battenkill still tumbles almost a half mile downward from the highest sources in Vermont to the Hudson River just above Schuylerville. The most spectacular waterfall is the seventy-five-foot drop, just west of Middle Falls, known as Dionondahowa. A walkway through the woods is accessible from Windy Hill Road near the Washington County fairgrounds. There, the hiker can watch the water roar into the Devil's Cauldron and surge down a steep gorge. The high falls have always presented a barrier to anadromous fish, so that even before anyone built a dam or polluted the river, there were never any runs of shad, herring, sturgeon, or salmon above this level. So if the Indian name Dionondahowa means *she opens the door for them*, whoever she is, she apparently isn't opening the door to fish.

THE NAME

How the Battenkill came by its name is an unsolved mystery. Anyone who has traveled through New York will have noticed any number of kills: Wallkill, Plattekill, Poestenkill, Catskill, Fish Kill, and on and on, all derived from the Dutch word for stream. Apparently everybody knows about this etymology except for a PETA spokesman named Anne Sullivan, who said the following about the town of Fishkill in 1996: "It seems like a lighthearted subject at first. But the real issue behind the name of Fishkill is the violent imagery."(5) Faced with this horrifying accusation, the mayor of Fishkill town refused to change the name, possibly the last occasion in which a public official has not caved in to ridiculous complaints. Fortunately, no humorless Battens have come forward to claim that the name Battenkill is an incitement to assassinate members of their family.

Just where the Batten part comes from is actually the puzzle. The late John Merwin (6) reported that researchers at the New Netherlands Project in Albany suggested "Batavia Kill" as the original name. There is a Batavia, New York, not in close proximity to the Kill. Certainly the Dutch liked to identify themselves as descendants of the Batavi, a Germanic tribe living on an island in the lower Rhine. This association was important as the Dutch began forming a national identity and foundational myth after their eighty-year war (1566-1648) for independence from the Habsburg Empire. (7)

Another writer, Esther Swift, (8) claimed that the river was named after an early settler named Bart. Local historian Tisha Dolton cites an answer provided by Tim Tefft, former editor of *The Greenwich Journal* and a descendant of the first settler in Greenwich. Tim's response elaborates Swift's: "I can find no proof that Bart or Bat Van Hogeboom ever lived at the mouth of the Battenkill, but genealogies list a number of Bartholomew/Bartholomus Van Hogebooms who were born in towns along the Hudson from the early to mid 1700's; one of them was baptized at Albany in 1702. There is a tradition of an early 1700's community along the Hudson near the mouth of the Battenkill. If it existed, perhaps Bart Hogeboom was among the settlers." Tim also noted that the name of the Bottskill Baptist Church in Greenwich seems to derive from "Bart's Kill." (9) Language is slippery.

On the Salem Road, Greenwich, N. Y.

Salem Road (top)
looking west towards Greenwich, NY
photo circa 1900
collection of Guy Arthur Barber

Salem Road (bottom)
just outside of East Greenwich, NY
postcard circa 1900
collection of Guy Arthur Barber

HISTORY

NATIVE NAMES

Aboriginal names are even more suspect. Bonnie Hoag cites William Beauchamp's *Aboriginal Place Names of New York*, which lists "Di-on-on-dah-o-wa Falls. Lower Falls on the Batten Kill near and above the devil's Cauldron, Galesville. This name seems the original of the preceding, and Sylvester applies it to the Batten Kill near Fort Miller. It was written Dionondehowe in 1709, and properly belongs to the creek. A. Cusick defined it *she opens the door for them*."(10) Beauchamp also mentions the more commonly applied name Ondawa in a more limited context: "On-da-wa was a name for White Creek in the town of the same name. A. Cusick defined this *coming again*."(11) Other interpretations of Ondawa include, according to Merwin, *white stream* or *country of rounded hills*, with the latter considered "probably more accurate." Voted least likely to catch on is the Mahican name "Tyetilegogtakook", *country around the river of toads*, which might be easier to say if a Mahican linguist could just simplify it to *river of toads*. It is a pity that this colorful name is not more popular.

The Battenkill River at Greenwich, N. Y.

The Trestle Bridge at Greenwich, NY
old postcard circa 1906
collection of Fannie Stevens

A VANISHED PARK

The great falls were a major attraction years ago. Dan Shaw (12) recalls the stories that his neighbor Lottie Bates used to tell about the park below the falls:

"Lottie Bates lived right around the corner, born and raised. Born in the house she was. She was in her nineties when she passed away, but she had very vivid memories and told me a lot of stories about the park. You know where you can park [on Windy Hill Road] and walk down to the falls? Well, there's a wooden fence across at

Hudson Valley Ry. crossing the Battenkill, Ondawa Park between Greenwich & Thomson, N.Y.

Trolley over Dionondahowa Falls (left)
This trolley would take people to the popular Dionondahowa Falls for picnics and swimming during the late 1800's and early 1900s.
old postcard circa 1900

Dionondahowa Falls (bottom)
postcard of a man fishing;
notice the trolley bridge at the top.
circa 1900.
collection of Fannie Stevens

Dionondahowa Falls, Greenwich, N. Y.

the last look-out. That path was a narrow road that kept going down, and there was a huge park down in there. It was owned by the mill across the river, and you got to it by trolley. The mill was quite prosperous years ago, and they sent over electricity, and there was power on this side. There was a pavilion. There was a ball field. People would go there for cookouts and bring their horse and buggy and drive down in there. In the winter time when the snow is on the ground, or in early spring before the foliage comes out, you can see the old road. It goes right past where you have to stop and winds right on down. If you go down, you'll hit the trolley tracks, and the road goes left. They've logged it twice; you'd have a hard time finding it. There's nothing hardly left down there, a couple of old cement piers, and I found an insulator one time. But it's all grown up, nothing to look at." Nature does not take long to reclaim abandoned land. Dan told us, "If we were gone, fifty years from now they say you wouldn't even be able to find the Northway. Trees grow right up through the cracks and shade it over. Then the wind blows the leaves all over it, and you get grass growing on it."

The Battenkill
looking south off Hill Farm Road
Sunderland, VT
Seline Skoug Photography

2. LIFE ON THE BATTENKILL

A COMPOSER'S MEMORIES

Bob Warren is a musician (13) and long-time resident of Greenwich, New York. We asked him how the river inspired him. The following is his meditation on this topic:

"I moved to Greenwich when I was sixteen, and that in itself was a big change for me because I was coming from an urban environment, living on Staten Island. I remember that I used to walk up Salem Street, and particularly at night, because at night in the warm weather there would be this fragrance. I don't know what it is to this day but always assumed it was some fern or flowering thing along the river that was very perfume-y but almost too much, almost overpowering. It was just mysterious to me. (14)

"And then of course there was the beach, and that was the place to immerse yourself in the river, and that we used to do at night. There was no fence. And you would have that feeling of slipping into the water when you couldn't really see the distinction between the water and the blackness of the night. And if the temperature was right, there wasn't much distinction between the water temperature and the air temperature, so you were just in this middle-land between sky and water. It's always had that pull for me.

"I've always felt that rivers are a conduit of ideas and emotions. Not only people's garbage, their wastes, flow down and work their way to the ocean but also their handy-work, their crafts. It's flowing, as though I look and see what's upstream and what's downstream, and it's always moving; it never stops. All that long line of particles and energy-transfers from Vermont to the Atlantic Ocean is in continuity, as though if you stepped on one end of it, the other end would respond.

"So when I wrote the music about Susan B. Anthony, my first thought was that she had lived on the river, and that fact had somehow allowed her to be great. She recognized that although she lived in this little hamlet, that the river went to other places, and she would eventually do that as well."

The Battenkill

Nestled between two ridges
Flowing down from the Green
   Mountain State
Its cold water rushes
Over beds of shale and slate

The English and the Irish
And the Scots and Dutchmen came
Awestruck by its beauty
Ondowa was its name

And when the rain falls…
And springtime melts the snow…
Each droplet becomes
Part of the river's flow

It was dreams that brought them here
And the wheel turned 'round and 'round
And the power of the water
Built the mills that built this town

They came seeking freedom
And to make their own way
It's the same thing that lives in
The hearts of people today

And when the rain falls
And springtime melts the snow
Each droplet becomes
Part of the river's flow

And though things are always changing
I hope some things never will
Like the way we welcome strangers to our
Little village on the Battenkill

Music and lyric by Bob Warren © 2004

A PHOTOGRAPHER'S TALE

Herb Eriksson and his wife Doris live on a hill overlooking the Camden Creek valley. Their farm, which extends on both sides of the creek, has been in the family for 84 years. Herb's parents emigrated from Sweden. His father, a cabinet maker, worked in New York City. The business was successful, but when Herb was nine years old, medical concerns brought about a change of plans. "I was very sickly," Herb explained. "I had something wrong with my heart. They said I wouldn't live unless I got out in the country, away from the city, to the fresh air. So they moved up here. My father knew nothing about farming. There were twenty milking cows and a barn full of young ones. He thought he could make a living up here. But what are you going to do as a fine cabinet maker up here in the country? So he started his own business fixing old houses. I started going to a one-room school house about a mile up the valley." Because the best cabinetry jobs were away over in Vermont, Herb soon took over running the dairy operation.

Doris was an early visitor to the Eriksson farm, one of many Swedish children in the city whose mothers sent their children to stay with Herb's mother Linnea in the fresh country air. At one time, there were sixteen children staying with the Eriksson family. Every year, Doris would come up for the summer, but as Herb was nine

years older, neither of them took any notice of the other until her senior year of high school, when she came to the farm for Easter. By then, as Herb says, "She had blossomed." In love and determined to leave the farm, Herb went to work for his father's former partners, who promised to make him an even better cabinet maker than his father was. The old partner was as good as his word, and Herb excelled. Still he was not satisfied; so he went back to school to be an architect and eventually developed a freelance design business for custom woodwork. Able to work from home, he moved back to the farm for good in 1988 and now lives in a house that he gradually built with his own hands, starting in 1971. The Battenkill watershed has been an inspiring subject for Herb's favorite hobby, photography; and his images of the river have found their way into many publications. The legendary fly tyer Doctor Lew Oatman and Shushan postmaster Al Prindle (15) were Herb's friends and appeared in many of his photos. Norman Rockwell himself lived just up the road, in Arlington, Vermont, and liked to use the cheerful postmaster as a model. Dr. Oatman even named one of his most famous bucktail fishing flies the "Shushan Postmaster."(16) Prindle died in 1947 and Oatman in 1958, but their memory lives on in Herb Eriksson's reminiscences and photos, and of course in the lore of the trout stream.

Looking towards Arlington, VT
Route 313, the Battenkill is on the right, circa 1955
photography, Herb Eriksson

THE TACKLE BOX

David and Joanne Fuller own a little house that used to be The Tackle Box store on the very edge of the Battenkill in Shushan, New York. It was in this shop that the fabled fly fishermen of yore met to buy tackle and swap yarns. Elizabeth remembers her father bringing her there when she was a little girl. On the walls are photographs of the place taken in the 1950's by photographer Herb Eriksson, including the iconic view looking in through the shop window. Old timers still show up to reminisce, and they have helped the Fullers to identify the people in the photos.

Roy and Ann Brown opened The Tackle Box in 1948. Joanne learned from Ann Brown's sister, Margaret Buffum, "The origin of the building is that this was known as Lucy's House. Lucy was a pig, and this was a pig barn. It was up in Murray Hollow, and they trucked it down here somehow." Later, Al Wiles owned the building as a fishing camp. In 1978, Al Wiles sold The Tackle Box to David's father.

The Fullers have been married 48 years and have fished the Battenkill since David's father first brought them here in 1964. David acquired the property in 1996 after his father died. A skilled carpenter and builder, David lovingly restored the old building, which was in a state of disrepair. There were squirrels living in the ceiling. David recalls, "We took wheelbarrow loads of nuts and stuff out of the ceiling."

Making frequent visits to the camp, the Fullers became friendly with the neighbors. The resulting personal ties and the appeal of the natural beauty of the place led the Fullers to retire here. Six months of the year, they live in The Tackle Box, and the rest of the year they live in a house up the road. It is appropriate that this building should be home to an avid fisherman. David said, "I fly-fish almost every night in the river. It's all catch and release."

The camp survived Tropical Storm Irene. David told us, "Everything was flooded except for this camp." Joanne recalled, "There were huge trees floating down the river, barreling down, with root balls that were maybe nine or ten feet in diameter."

The main kinds of flotsam coming down the river in the summer are canoes, kayaks, and tubes. David often steps forward to help those in obvious distress. "One day we could hear some people yelling. There was a man, his wife, a young kid, and a baby. Pretty soon their canoe tipped over, and they all jumped out, and the canoe righted itself, and it was just the little baby in the swamped canoe going down the river. So I'm not a great swimmer, but I jumped in and caught the canoe and got the baby out. The mother was just terrorized. They told me, 'That's it. We'll never get in another canoe.'"

Life is never dull at The Tackle Box.

PAINTING THE WATERSHED

White Creek flows through the village of Salem, New York on its way to Black Creek, which carries its waters to the Battenkill. Beside this clear stream is the studio of one of America's premier landscape artists, Harry Orlyk. On a cool May morning, smoke rose from the stove pipe in the roof of the little frame building where he finishes his masterpieces. The interior was well lit, even on this cloudy day, by windows and a skylight. Several paintings hung on the wall, awaiting finishing touches. They looked perfect to me already, but Harry pointed out where they need to be tweaked.

All of these paintings were brought to near-completion on site, or *en plein air*, as artists say. Outdoor painting can be a grueling occupation, what with sun, rain, wind, heat, and cold. Harry Orlyk has found a way to make the job a little easier: he often paints inside his van, sitting in the driver's seat, with a c-clamp holding the artwork to the steering wheel. His palette sits on the passenger seat. It is a large rectangular board with 1x3 sidewalls because he uses a lot of paint. His colors are those of the spectrum, with no earth tones; and for the last two years, he has used no ultramarine blue. He paints on the finest Belgian linen, which he staples to pieces of wallboard. The finished paintings go to the gallery with the wallboard attached. When asked about this curious way of presenting his creations, he explains that he does not want to waste time and energy doing anything that takes him away from communing with the land.

> **"Each painting entails facing a swath of creation and observing something of its story"**

As he explained in the introduction to a recent event at the Laffer Gallery, "A quarter century of painting has been an act of the imagination to determine who and what I am with respect to the earth and sky. Process, rather than product oriented, searching for the daily painting, has become a way of living in relationship with the earth.

The River Spirit
silver pendant
Bonnie Hoag, silversmith

To become a human being, part of nature rather than separately observing it from the outside, like hunter-gatherers, I am led from one opportunity to the next, being directed by seasonal stages. The relationship has become the trust I give it to show me where my next painting will be. Each painting entails facing a swath of creation and observing something of its story, becomes a long log of small truths."(17)

A SANCTUARY

Bonnie Hoag's property in Shushan, New York embraces the river both physically and in name. Dionondehowa Wildlife Sanctuary and School comprises 217 acres along the western shore of the Battenkill. We visited Bonnie on a cold, windy day in April. A few snowflakes blew by as we gazed out past her red barn to the blue Vermont hills. She spoke at length of the spiritual connection that she feels with the land, which inspired her and co-founder Geoffrey Ovington to buy the property. The nonprofit forever-wild land trust attempts to provide "an opportunity to rethink our relationship with the land and our basic economic principle of 'land as commodity.'"

"The land, then, can become a most trusted teacher… when we pause on it, quiet ourselves, and open our senses… we open to a larger, unprescribed experience of what it means to be alive, to be human - individually wrapped quanta in an infinite, undulating, atomized reality. We're not *on* a magic carpet. We ARE the magic carpet."(18)

THE PARTY LINE

Charlie Tracy (19) grew up in Center Falls. He related one of his many childhood adventures.

"Back in those days, the mill in Center Falls was called the Blandy Paper Company, and there was a pile of houses, it must have been fifteen, twenty houses, and down by me there were a lot of homes too, and the people who lived there all worked at the mill. And all the homes were owned by the mill. My home wasn't, and the Perkins' home wasn't, but all the others were. The mill ran twenty-four hours a day. We were just kids then. I was eight or ten. George [Perkins] was a little older. I think it was George and I, Frankie Colby, and Eddie Dutcher who were in on this adventure. Back then, we all had eight-party lines, so we could hear other people's conversations. Well, there was this one lady who worked there who had a major set of [assets]. This lady, who lived near the mill, said something that Frankie overheard about a *rendezvous*. So Frankie told me, 'There's gonna be some action on the back road. There's gonna be a *rendezvous*.' This is on that Old Center Falls Road, in Cozy Hollow. So we all got on our bikes. Now, you guys remember the streamers on the bicycles, and how we used to put baseball cards with clothespins to buzz against the spokes? Well, we're all pedaling down the road, and we all hook up at the four corners right there. Then we saw this lady take off, and down the road she goes, so we pedaled our bicycles; and we stopped when we saw this guy get out of his car. She gets led off, and up into the woods they go. And we're sneaking up after them. I was scared to death! This man was a big guy, and he'd frickin' kill us! It was right up off the road, directly across the river from the paper mill. We're being as quiet as we can, and they're hugging and kissing and grabbing. And Frankie — I swear he got up real close — he wasn't more than twenty yards from them. Then we started laughing; we couldn't help it, because we'd never seen anything quite like that. And they heard us, so Frankie took off, and we took off and pedaled our bicycles back home. I'll never forget it, but those were the days when you knew what everybody else was doing because of those party lines."

A GIFT OF LAND

In the fall of 2015, The Battenkill Conservancy received a generous gift of waterfront property on the Kill from the Schmidt family. We met G. Latimer ("Lat") Schmidt in Cambridge to talk about his memories of his family's camp. His father, an engineer at General Electric, lived in Schenectady and bought a 10.8-acre plot of land downriver from East Greenwich in 1973. The site appealed to him because he was an avid fly fisherman and a supporter of Trout Unlimited. There he constructed a small cabin of rough-cut lumber from a local sawmill. Most of the lot lies in the flood plain between the railroad track and the river, and the cabin is raised up on treated posts. Even so, flood water has washed across its floor more than once. This intermittent flooding keeps the soil fertile, and the moist loam along the river bank supports a forest of ferns up to six feet tall. Dutchman's breeches and trout lilies bloom on the shore in the spring.

We asked what prompted the family to donate the land to the Conservancy. Lat explained, "My mother died in 2012, and my father's health declined. He's in assisted living but doing remarkably well for a 91-year-old. The family looked at his assets, and he has enough to see him through. We didn't want to sell the land to just anybody. It would be terrible to have somebody come in and clear it down to the water's edge. We were happy to be able to see the land kept natural. The scenery of the countryside around here is so exquisite."

Icy Battenkill
acrylic on board
Jacob Houston

AN ARTIST'S FAMILY

Jim and Claire Houston and their son, artist Jacob Houston,(20) live about fifty yards from the Battenkill, on Trout Brook, a sparkling perennial stream that tumbles through their property on its way to the Kill. When we visited them one April morning in their spotlessly tidy home, the morning sunlight twinkled on the brook, and the liquid green ribbon of the river shone through the bare tree limbs. Jim, a civil engineer, takes solace from the water.

"I'm out on the river every morning and evening," he told us. Every day he sees some kind of wildlife. There are many beavers, making their huts of sticks or burrowing into the bank. Sometimes the burrows undercut the land so much that whole trees fall in when the river rises and its waters rush through the rodents' tunnels. Minks are also active along the bank. These sleek little members of the weasel clan like to hunt muskrats and can wipe out a whole muskrat colony.

Archaeological mysteries crop up, such as the light gold ceramic tiles on the river bottom from Center Falls to mid-way up to Battenville. They are a reminder that houses and mills have come and gone. Some vanished almost without a trace. In Center Falls, there used to be numerous houses for the mill workers, a hotel, bar, and gas station, now all gone. Numerous open wells were left behind, traps for the unwary. When a boy named Jaliek Rainwalker went missing in November of 2007, the police probed the abandoned wells (or as many as they could find) and partially filled them in. The fate of Jaliek is still unknown.(21)

More than one ghost roams the valley. Below the Hollingsworth and Vose paper mill was an island known as Spook Island. Nobody talks about it anymore, now that it has united with the south bank and grown up with trees. Apparently the spooks have cleared out too.

Hazards, natural or supernatural, seldom deterred local youngsters from jumping into the stream. The Eagleville and Rexleigh covered bridges were favorite jumping-in spots. Numerous rope swings are still to be found, and the clear cool water attracts swarms of inner-tubers in the summer. The water is more inviting than it used to be. Claire remembers that when she was a child there were so many pollutants that the floor of the river below Battenville was crusted white, and "your skin would tingle when you went into the water. The mills discharged big algae-like masses of gunk, varying in color according to what they were making. Mostly, they discharged at night so people wouldn't see it."

The Houstons recall that above the dam at Battenville, people used to harvest ice from the river to stock their ice houses. In the old days, the ice used to get so thick that huge blocks would explode from the river at the spring thaw. Don Perkins, who lived just a short way above the dam in Center Falls, planted weeping willows along the bank to keep the ice blocks from flying out and hitting his house.

When darkness had hidden everything but the campfire and the faces around it, the ghost stories began. . .

A TERRIFYING TALE

Camping by the river was a yearly treat for the Greenwich school children. Bob Barber made his property available, and teachers from Greenwich Central School would chaperone the children and instruct them about nature and camping skills. Bob taught them how to boil water without a pot. At night, students and teachers alike would take turns telling ghost stories. When darkness had hidden everything but the campfire and the faces around it, Ken Sheffield always told the following story:

"We used to camp out here a long time ago with the kids like this. And one time after we had all gone to bed, Mr. Pemrick and I were in our tent here. The kids up in the last tent started yelling 'Help! Help! Mr. Pemrick, Mr. Sheffield, come and help us,' as if there were something really wrong. Of course we knew they were pulling our leg. So I'd go up to see, and they'd all laugh. Then I'd get back in the tent, into my sleeping bag, and the same thing happened all over again. Well, this went on about four times, and finally we said, 'That's it. We're not going back. Let 'em make noise.' So the next morning we got up, and all the kids were having breakfast. We made fresh pancakes cooked on the grill, and all the kids were in line eating, and we said, 'Where are the kids from the last tent? They aren't here.'

"So I got up, and I looked, and I could see there was a big rip in the tent. And there were drag marks to the river, but we never found those kids who were in that last tent."

Asked whether the stories calmed the children down, Ken replied, "No, they all went kind of crazy after that, and we had to calm them down."

To this day, those camp-outs on the Battenkill, with swimming, hiking, and scary stories, are among the fondest memories of that generation of Greenwich alumni.

Mill Hollow, Greenwich, NY
kids jumping off old abandoned bridge
abutments into the Battenkill
Cliff Oliver, phtography

THE HIGH JUMP

Many of our friends tell tales of jumping into the river from the railroad trestle. This daredevil feat pales next to Dan Shaw's story of a high jump.

"At the Stevens & Thompson paper mill site, before the hydroelectric installation went in, we used to go swimming. And I'm talking about the early '80's, when we were young, but we were all adults. On the side that the hydro's on, there was a sheer cliff. And we used to go around and climb up it, and you could jump off. Now, we weren't kids; we were in our thirties and forties, so we knew better than to do it. And it's so funny we'd all be daring each other even at that age to go do it.

**"You just have to
know how to do it.
Cross your arms and
remember to plug
your nose..."**

"You could jump off the cliff at forty to fifty feet, and then there was another spot up higher — it took a while to get up there — and it was almost a hundred feet high. I got up to fifty feet and said, 'This is as far as I'm going. I don't know if I can even do this.' But I built up enough courage, and I jumped in. You just have to know how to do it. Cross your arms and remember

to plug your nose because you'll hit so hard that it drives water up your nose, and you'll come out gagging and choking. You also have to remember, the minute you hit the water, you've got to push your feet forward like a fin, and it'll bring you around so you're upside-down in the water, and you're not going down; you're going back up. Then you just flip around and come up.

"So we dared each other, and a bunch of us jumped off at fifty feet. Three of them went up to a hundred feet, and two did jump. They were athletic people, and they were all 'gameys' anyway. One of the fellows climbed up there, and it took a heck of a job to get up, and he couldn't jump. Well, it was even harder to get back down, because you couldn't see your toe holds.

"Of the two who jumped, I don't remember about the first one, but here's the funny thing that happened to the second one. You had to wear an old pair of sneakers because you were climbing on rocks, and it's all ledgy up there. Well, when he came down, he hit so hard in his old sneakers that his feet went right through 'em, and the sneakers were up to his knees."

ROMANCE ON THE RIVER

Ken and Judy Flagg (22) live in Salem, New York, close to Black Creek. They met for the first time beside the Battenkill in 1965. Judy told us, "I was 15 years old and lived in East Greenwich, and my parents' house was on the Battenkill. My next-door neighbor Emily Jones was also 15, and we had for several years seen two boys come to the field in front of our houses and pitch tents, sometimes in the snow!"

Ken: "Every year we would come up there. We would skip school and come up from Colonie."

Judy: "Which we considered to be the big city. City boys. And this particular year we saw two tents go up on the first day of fishing, which was April first. And so Emily says, 'Let's go down there and talk to those boys.' Now you've got to understand, Emily was a little more aggressive than I was, but she persuaded me to come along.

"So we go down to the first tent, and these two boys came out. One was a short little stocky guy with fuzzy brown hair, little cherub kind of face, and yack-box, talk, talk, talk."

Ken: "That was Lenny."

Judy: "And this other, taller, blond hair, with those black-rimmed glasses that everybody was wearing in 1965, and he came out of the tent, saw us, didn't say a word, picked up his fishing rod and headed for the river! And I thought, what's his problem? And then I thought, we shouldn't be talking to these boys; they're just too sophisticated for us. They just don't want to talk to these country bumpkins. So we talked a little bit more to this Lenny, and then we decided we'd go to the next tent. And we thought the two tents were together."

Ken: "I don't know who those guys were."

Judy: "And they were very nice and talkative, and we stayed for about ten minutes. Then we took off. But that was our first encounter. Ken didn't say anything to us. I thought he was a conceited city boy."

Ken: "Fishing time was precious. I'd gotten a really nice trout a little earlier, of which those other two guys were really envious. They wanted to know where I caught it, so of course I told them the wrong place."

Judy: "Fast forward 35 years. I had come back from wherever I was, and being an alto sax player, I joined the Washington County band. My daughter Caitlin also played alto sax, so I brought her along. Well, next to me was this French-horn player, and I was just sort of checking him out because he was not bad looking-- sort of a Nick Nolte chiseled face-- and he wasn't wearing a wedding ring. So I said to Caitlin, 'What do you think of the French-horn player?' She leans forward and looks and says, 'Go for it, Mom!'"

Ken: "So I asked her out for a cup of coffee."

Judy: "At Stewart's in Cambridge, and we order the coffee, and he looks at me and says, 'I don't have any money.' I thought, Ooh! This is a class act, so I cough up the money for the coffees, and we go and sit down, and we start talking, and he asks where I'm from; and I say, 'East Greenwich.' And he says, 'I know where that is!' And I'm thinking, he doesn't know where East Greenwich is. He thinks I'm saying East Greenbush because everybody always confuses the two, and that's down by Albany.' So I said, 'East *Greenwich*', and he said, 'Yes, my friend and I

used to go camping there.' And I must have got this deer in the headlights look, and he said, 'You weren't one of those girls that came to our tent in 1965, were you?' I said, 'Yes! And you were the blond one who ran off and wouldn't talk to us!'"

Ken: "Well, I was shy at 15 and wasn't interested in girls yet."

Judy: "Anyway, by the time we were having this conversation, we had both been divorced for about 13 years, and neither of us was really looking for anyone. So we were drinking our coffee, and Ken

asked me whether I was going to go to the cider fest party. I said yes, and he said, 'Well, I've decided that at this point in my life I just need to be alone.' What kind of mixed message was that? 'Are you going to the party? I need to be alone.' But we both decided to go anyway, and it was a horse-drawn carriage ride, and that was it: we just clicked."

Ken: "You invited me to dinner."

Judy: "And he brought his dog on the first date."

Ken: "I brought my dog, and I also brought her a bird's nest and a bottle of wine."

Battenkill Serenity (top)
acrylic on board
Jacob Houston

Judy: "He was *late* for dinner. We must have been discussing that I collected nests. It was an interesting one, a bobolink; they're on a stalk and low to the ground. And I looked into the living room, and his dog was *on my sofa*."

Ken: "I figured if she didn't like the dog, it wasn't going to work."

Judy: "And we've been together ever since."

LIFE ON THE BATTENKILL

A WRITER'S LIFE

James Howard Kunstler (23) is an author, artist, and resident of Greenwich, New York.

"I first came up here in 1973. I'd just got a job at the evening newspaper in Albany, New York. It was called the *Knickerbocker News*, and it was an old, esteemed paper that had been acquired by Hearst and then kind of run into the ground for the last couple of decades of its life. I was there a couple of decades before it actually folded up its tent like every evening newspaper in America. But anyway, I worked there, and I started coming up to Saratoga, and I started coming out to Washington County. I had developed an interest in fly fishing a couple of years earlier, in my early twenties,

and I understood that the Battenkill was a great fly fishing stream. And I spent a bit of time there during the period I was actually working a day job and wasn't as free as I later became.

"So I was hired to go to a glamor job in California working for *Rolling Stone* magazine, and I couldn't turn that down. So I went out there, and I didn't like the job very much, and after about a year I started trying to engineer a way to get out of there and get out of the business of being a salary mule for a corporation. And I was getting up at four o'clock in the morning to write a horror novel, and I did! It was eventually published by a kind of a cheap, pulpy, horror paperback line under the title of *The Hunt*. But it was actually titled, as a working title, *Bagging Bigfoot*.

"I had read *Jaws* in 1975, and I was quite sure I could write a better horror novel than Peter Benchley. So I tried. And I got an agent very quickly, and I developed this delusion that I was going to become an instant millionaire. So I was still in San Francisco at the time, and I was going down to Van Ness Avenue, which is the car dealer street in the city of San Francisco, pricing out Jensen Interceptors and other exotic sports cars because I thought I was just going to hit the jackpot. And nothing happened. My agent kind of sent it out, and nothing happened, nothing happened. I was determined to get out of San Francisco, and all I had was a motorcycle. So I sold all my chattels and rode the motorcycle across the country. Stopped in Washington, D.C. for about five months, where a former girlfriend of mine lived. She was living in an apartment with two other girls, and I stopped there because I thought that the sale of my novel was imminent and I would become that instant millionaire, and then I could figure out what I was going to do.

"But the days went by, and the days went by, and my agent told me to rewrite the novel. I was in this row house in Georgetown, pretty posh, and my former girlfriend had become a TV producer in Washington; so she was doing pretty well. And she had two roommates. One of them was a very beautiful lady lawyer who also happened to be a nymphomaniac. So that was pretty interesting for a while, except I made the mistake of falling in love with her. Big mistake. But in the meantime, to keep body and soul together, I got a job driving a cab in D.C., and I did that for about four months, which was really very demoralizing. By the time winter rolled around I was completely discouraged. I fired my agent, who had failed to sell this book and make me an immediate over-night sensation millionaire, and I returned to upstate New York.

"I came back to where I had started but in a very different situation. I was now a starving bohemian. I had made a deliberate decision when I left *Rolling Stone* that this was as far as I was going to get in journalism, and I was going to drop out and write books—novels really, because that

was the programming for people with literary aspirations in the seventies. So my horror novel wasn't selling, but I just put that aside and started doing other things. So I landed in Saratoga, got an apartment, which was a pretty nice apartment for a guy who was a starving bohemian. I got a job working as a goon in the mental health ward of the hospital. I basically held people down for their Thorazine shots and took blood pressures and made notes.

"At the time, I was still really infatuated with trout fishing, and I was so glad to be out of the city, and I was so glad to be in basically a main-street country town that I returned to trout fishing with a vengeance. About eighteen months after my return to Saratoga, my first novel got accepted. It was a story about kids in a summer camp. It was kind of a juvenile, beginner's novel, but I got paid for it. And I took about a third of the advance that I got, and I bought a really good Orvis bamboo fly rod. These were the last years of the bamboo fly rod being state-of-the-art, before they introduced graphite. And I just used the hell out of it. I used it on Kayaderosseras Creek which runs through Saratoga County, but I also spent a lot of time in Washington County, spooking around the Battenkill and learning it and figuring it out. It was much more difficult to fish for esoteric reasons having to do with the nature of fly fishing and the nature of the river itself because it's not really a free-stone creek

like a babbling brook with pools and riffs. It's very flat water that's generally not very interrupted, and the trout can see you coming from a gazillion miles away, and you have to be a good hunter to fish for them, as well as being very knowledgeable about the insect life, because they're not easily fooled. But it was so beautiful to be there that I didn't care that much about how well or badly I was catching trout. I just liked being out there. And I did catch trout now and again, enough to stimulate me. So that was my introduction to the Battenkill. I still had that motorcycle, and I got a couple of pipe clamps, and I used to clamp the aluminum rod case to the rack on the back of my motorcycle and ride out here. "So I did that for years and years and years; and by and by, beginning in the eighties, I became interested again in painting, which was something that I had done as a young person. So I returned to that, and I discovered that I was much more interested in going out with a French easel than a fly rod. That's still pretty much the situation, but I do still occasionally go out with a fly rod and pretend that I'm going to catch fish. And even when I do catch them, I let them go. Now as an elderly gentleman, I still go down there and fish."

Kayaking on the Battenkill (left)
oil on canvas (plein air)
James H. Kunstler

WILD
TROUT
OF THE
BATTENKILL

Brook Trout

Brown Trout

3. ENVIRONMENT

ABOUT TROUT

Outdoor writers have made the Battenkill famous as a trout stream. Fame has its drawbacks, though, and some fear that more fishermen may lead to fewer fish. Our friends who fished the New York portion of the river fifty years ago report that even though the water was dirtier then, the fishing was much better. Why? Everybody has a reason. Parts of the river have silted in, and the shallower water is not cool enough. Mergansers are eating the fish, and nobody eats mergansers. Osprey and bald eagles take a share.

Brown trout (*Salmo trutta*) are imports from Europe. The common name of the fish belies its attractive coloration, ranging from silvery to bronze, with a variable pattern of spots, which provide camouflage against the pebbles of the river bottom. Anglers serious about their art tie artificial lures to resemble emerging aquatic insects, but trout are not averse to earthworms, frogs, or whatever else they can catch, especially small fish.

A less common catch is the beautiful native brook trout (*Salvelinus fontinalis*), surely a trouty-looking animal but more closely related to the northerly fish known as charr. Like mature brown trout, the brook trout has well-flavored pink flesh similar to salmon, and both belong to the family Salmonidae, which includes salmon, trout, charrs, and whitefishes. All of these fishes share a number of features including absence of spiny fin rays and presence of an adipose fin, that soft, fleshy and apparently useless appendage on the back of a trout between the dorsal fin and the tail. The charr and true trout clans are thought to have split off from a common ancestor in the Ogligocene, some 30 million years ago. Charr (and brookies) have a boat-shaped vomer, which is a bone in the roof of the mouth, with small teeth at its crest. Such small distinctions are the stuff of taxonomy. Dr. Samuel Latham Mitchill, a New York physician, professor of natural history, and sometime politician, named the brook trout in a book published in 1814, assigning the fish to the genus *Salmo*. More careful observation by the English biologist John Richardson in 1836 resulted in reassignment to the genus *Salvelinus*. It took a while for anglers to get used to the name change. The editor of *Forest and Stream*, Charles Hallock, was so moved that he wrote a poem beginning "I am Salmo fontinalis" and concluding, "Yet they call me Salvelinus./ Can you fancy sin more heinous?"(24)

Trout Lily

Wild Trout of the Battenkill (left)
Trout lily (above)
watercolors
Elizabeth Cockey

FOREIGN INVADERS

Walking along the bank or kayaking down the stream, rounding a bend to behold a pristine stretch of water and wilderness, it is a pleasant fantasy to imagine that the waterway must have appeared just so to the Indians or seventeenth-century explorers. Yet the vegetation is in many cases quite different from what a visitor would have seen a few hundred years ago. Chestnut trees, which predominated in many of the eastern woodlands, have succumbed to blight. Elm trees, also blight-stricken, seldom grow large. But the change is not limited to the absence of once-dominant species. Many of the most common plants here are newcomers from other continents.

Those lovely spires of purple flowers along the river bank are purple loosestrife (*Lythrum salicaria*), brought in from Europe as an ornamental and as a pollen source for honey bees. Non-serrated, opposite leaves and a square stem distinguish it from other similar plants. Despite its attractive appearance, it clogs waterways and displaces other plant varieties, reducing biodiversity. Since

government biologists have imported several loosestrife-eating insects, most notably beetles of the genus Gallerucella, the plant appears to be under fairly good control.

Another alien along the waterside is Japanese knotweed (*Fallopia japonica*). The stalks are hollow, with nodes like those seen on bamboo. The leaves are broad, pointed ovals, and clusters of upright white flowers appear in late summer. The tall weed crowds out other vegetation, then dies back in the winter, exposing the bank to erosion. The young shoots can be eaten like asparagus, but not many people are interested in gathering them. Josh Ness, an assistant professor at Skidmore College, is investigating a possible malign synergy between this weed and an introduced insect, the European fire ant (*Myrmica rubra*). The ants are fond of the sweet sap that exudes from any bruise or scrape on the knotweed, and they swarm over it, protecting it with their stingers from further damage by any other animal. Ness is concerned that such an interaction could set up an "invasional meltdown," resulting in rapid spread of a nasty stinging ant

and a noxious weed. Luring the ants with Chips Ahoy cookies, Ness and his students are on the case.(25)

Garlic mustard (*Alliaria petiolata*) is also extremely common. This biennial shows up the first year as a low plant with round leaves with lobulated edges. The next year, it shoots up to about three feet tall, with pointed, serrated leaves and a cluster of white flowers with four petals each. Brought over by the colonists as a food flavoring herb, it has spread wherever weeds grow. The roots of the plant are said to produce a chemical that inhibits the growth of the root fungi needed by other plants. White-tail deer leave it alone, so that it outcompetes plant species more palatable to deer. When it dies back in the winter, it leaves bare ground just like Japanese knotweed.

Daring diners on wild weeds advocate harvesting edible invasive plants for the table. Finding a large stand of garlic mustard in our back yard, I picked as much of it as I could stuff into a pot, discarded the tougher parts of the stems, and added enough water to come up about half way through the mass of green matter. Even the white flowers went into the pot. After

Wild Parsnips
from the roadside on
State Route 313, NY
Barton Cockey, photography

cooking the greens covered for half an hour, I drained off the water and added olive oil, salt, and paprika. The result was remarkably tasty; even our dinner guests claimed to like it. Picking the plants before the long, slender seed pods form will prevent re-seeding and should eventually eliminate the weed wherever it is thoroughly harvested. There are just two problems: it is hard to eliminate all the flower heads, and the critical areas along the river bank are difficult to reach and full of ticks.

Another, more attractive member of the mustard family is the sweet rocket or dame's rocket (*Hesperis matronalis*), which brightens the valley with numberless clusters of pink and white, four-petaled blooms in late May and early June. The U.S. Department of Agriculture considers it an invasive species, but it is one that I would miss if it disappeared.

Along the roads and in abandoned fields, the flat-topped, yellow flower clusters of wild parsnip (*Pastinaca sativa*) appear in late May and June. As with the cultivated variety, the roots are edible, but the sap in the leaves contains a substance that may cause a photosensitive skin reaction resembling a chemical burn. Do not roll around in the wild parsnips, even though they smell good.

Waders and swimmers in the Battenkill may run afoul of the dreaded rock snot (*Didymosphenia geminate*). No one will mistake this plant for an ornamental. Tan, brown, or white, it feels like wet wool, and despite its popular name, it is not slimy. The actual organism is a diatom, with a silica cell-wall. Branching extra-cellular stalks of polysaccharide and protein composition attach to rocks and

may cover the bed of a stream, interfering with other plants and animals. Although considered an invasive, this one-celled organism is actually native to North America but has extended its range over the last century. Unlike algae, which undergo harmful, oxygen-depleting blooms in response to increased nutrients, rock snot thrives in nutrient-poor waters, and oxygen levels among its matted stalks are actually increased. Because a single drop of water is enough to carry the diatom from one stream to another, boaters and fishermen are advised to clean and dry their equipment and avoid felt-soled waders.

Swimming in the "Kill"
Claire Houston, photography

A SPILL AT THE BEACH

It was a cloudy summer morning in 1969 at the community beach in Greenwich, a tranquil spot just off State Route 29. Smitty Wright (26) recalls the occasion:

"Paul Getty and I were on [lifeguard] duty. When we arrived, it was evident, even from the parking lot, that there was some kind of slick covering the whole of the Battenkill that we could see. It had a sheen and would change colors like oil. So there we were, and John Traver [the athletic coach who supervised the lifeguard program] was there shortly thereafter. He always checked in every morning. And he said we can't let anybody in the water. Number one, we weren't a hundred percent sure what was on the water. We assumed it came from one of the mills up the river. And that was back in the days when a lot of kids came unaccompanied on their bicycles, or parents even drove their children down and left them for a few hours at a time, and someone would come and retrieve them later. And John said, 'I'm going to see what I can find out; but you guys have to keep everybody out of the water.'

"I'm going to see what I can find out, but you guys keep everybody out of the water !"

"We did have to turn several people away. We waited and waited, and probably around one o'clock in the afternoon some men in dark suits appeared, from New Jersey, and stood there at the top of the sand. They certainly didn't walk through the water or the sand. Then they told Mr. Traver that they were going to Someplace Else [restaurant, now closed] to have lunch and discuss the matter further. Now by this time, there was still a slick and a sheen over all the water, but it wasn't quite as pronounced as it had been early in the morning. Whatever had let loose had either emptied or been shut off. Then John Brownell came down, as a lot of Paul's friends often did when they knew where he was. By this time it was a hot day, and we were thirsty. So John went and got some beer, and we sat in the shade and had a couple of cold beers while we waited to see what would happen.

"Then I remember they brought a guy down — he was supposedly an H&V [Hollingsworth and Vose] employee — I don't remember his name. He was a short man with dark hair, came down in his bathing suit with a couple of bales of hay in the back of a vehicle, and he used our rowboat. We strung a rope from the lifeguard's chair across the river to a tree and strung hay all along that rope to collect what was left that came down the river, which was little or nothing by that time. Then the next day, we pulled it out."

Elizabeth was there too. She had heard about the spill and came down to see. She and Smitty had just finished high school, and both served as lifeguards that summer. Elizabeth remembers the contrast between the 'half-naked teenagers" and the men in dark suits. A search of the Greenwich library files failed to turn up any contemporary news story about the spill. Shortly before she died, we asked Sally Tefft, whose family ran the local newspaper, why the official record is silent; and she suggested that the mishap must have occurred on a Wednesday after the paper had already gone to press.

Ironically, now that the river is crystal clear, fewer people use the beach. The only environmental contaminant is the excrement of resident geese that take advantage of the absence of bathers. Their droppings are the proof and guarantee of their claim as squatters.

ENVIRONMENT

A TALE OF TWO TURTLES

Snapping turtles live a long time and are not picky eaters. They feast on whatever they find: live fish, dead fish, vegetation, and filter-feeding mollusks. As a result, they concentrate environmental toxins in their tissues. Howard Romack, a retired science teacher (27) in Cambridge, New York, recalled how two snapping turtles helped to study pollution.

"When we were kids, we used to go down in the back of a local dump, and I remember seeing bulldozers pushing 55-gallon drums of who knows what down in there. Fast forward to 1985: the pathologist for the Department of Environmental Conservation (DEC) called me at the school and said, 'Would you collect a snapping turtle from the vicinity of that dump and then collect another one of about the same size (to keep our variables even) from a high-altitude pond where you don't have as much runoff?' So I did. And we had a technician come up and analyze those two turtles. He took them to Albany and removed muscle and fat and liver tissue and sent it to a lab to be analyzed. The computer readouts came back, and they were very heavy in a lot of chemical pesticides, mostly farm pesticides like Mirex and chlordane and lindane, those kinds of things that they were putting on the crops. But the PCB levels were also very high, unusually high. We were getting ready to put a little playground behind the school, but we decided that we didn't want the kids playing around back there until some more tests were done. Finally, they had the water tested back there, and fortunately the water tests appeared to be fine. But it's always a good idea to study animals that live in the water. Not only turtles but also aquatic filter feeders like fresh-water clams, caddisfly larvae, and the nymphs and larvae of other aquatic insects can tell us a lot about how clean the water is. The good news is that based on surveys of macroinvertebrates in the Battenkill, the river is in good health."

WINGED HARBINGERS

Though retired from teaching, Howard Romack maintains a particular interest in invertebrates, reptiles and amphibians. He shared the following story.

"Since about 1990, we've noticed a second flight of tiger swallowtail butterflies coming out in July, and it correlates nicely with a slight increase in degree days that we've been seeing on thermal data collectors along the Battenkill and up into southern Vermont. The long-term kind of study would be to try to figure out whether we have a double brood or whether in fact it's a crypto-species, one that looks like a tiger swallowtail but may be different. And so scientific colleagues are studying both groups of these butterflies and doing DNA analysis on them.

"We think what's happening is that slightly higher temperatures are allowing more southerly species to come into our area. Some of the butterflies that we see here that weren't here five or six years ago are ones that have been able to switch their host plants, one in particular being a large southern swallowtail *Papilio cresphontes*, that feeds on citrus, called the 'orangedog,' and up here it's been appearing on the coneflowers in July. And now we know that this butterfly has switched from citrus to pricklyash [*Zanthoxylum americanum*, the northernmost member of the citrus family]."

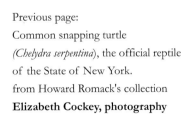

"We have a flight of a very fascinating moth. It's *Sthenopis auratus*, the golden ghost moth. The story behind that is interesting. I keep a black light behind my shed, to see what's flying and to collect a few things for showing to kids. I found a moth out there that I had never seen before. This was several summers ago. And I called Dr. McCabe at the New York State museum, and I said, 'Tim, I've found a species that I haven't seen before.' And he said, 'Describe it.' So I said, 'It's a beautiful, rusty, reddish-brown color with gold spots on its wings.' He said, 'That's *Sthenopis auratus*. Where did you find it?' I said, 'I found it at my light.'

"He came up that night! And he said, 'Let's go down and look at your ferns in the woods.' The biology of that moth had not been worked out, and it was an extremely rare moth. So we went down into the woods, and we spent until one o'clock in the morning looking at all the ferns, and he said, 'Well, we think it's a fern feeder.' So I got thinking about that. Patty had wanted some ferns for the yard, so I had gone up to Murray Hollow on the Battenkill and dug up some rootstocks and brought them back. Well, I went out with a head lamp, and lo and behold, there was a male fanning its pheromones. And we dug rootstocks and found the larvae. Tim and another colleague wrote the paper describing the life history of *Sthenopis auratus*. And that's where the discovery was made, right here in the valley of the Battenkill."(28)

Previous page:
Common snapping turtle
(*Chelydra serpentina*), the official reptile
of the State of New York.
from Howard Romack's collection
Elizabeth Cockey, photography

(Above)
1) Top left, Orangedog *(Papilio cresphontes)* female.
2) Top right, Dobsonfly *(Corydalis cornutus)* male.
   The fearsome pinchers are used in mating.
   Fish eat the aquatic larvae, known as hellgrammites.
3) Middle left, First flight tiger swallowtail, female,
   Once considered a subspecies of *Papiliio glaucus* but
   now classified as *Pterourus canadensis*.
4) Middle right, Second flight tiger swallowtail, female.
5) Bottom left, Golden ghost moth *(Sthenopis auratus)* male.
6) Bottom right, Golden ghost moth *(Sthenopis auratus)* female.

ENVIRONMENT

Ruins of Biotech Mills in 2016
Battenville, NY
Barton Cockey, Photography

ENVIRONMENT

BUSTING BIOTECH

Biotech Mills in Battenville, New York was a notorious polluter. Phil Gitlen, the environmental attorney responsible for shutting it down, related the story.

"It's interesting to me because everything that goes around comes around. I grew up on the Beaver Kill, with a fly rod in my hands when I was five and six years old. And so when I was enforcement counsel at the state DEC in 1977 and the enforcement referral came across for the *Batten* Kill, someplace I had never heard of before, I had no idea where it was, though I was spending a lot of time in Washington County at the GE plant at Fort Edward because I was handling the state's case against GE for PCB's. But the Battenkill was more interesting to me in a sense because it was a famed fly-fishing stream, and indeed I had an Orvis bamboo rod that I had just purchased, and it was the "Battenkill" model. So I was pretty interested in it.

"Biotech Mills (I'd never been there, never seen it) was on the Battenkill, which was interesting. It was pretty apparent from what I was reading that it was a really old plant that they had cob-jobbed into producing a toilet tissue product. It was owned by a guy named Marvin Ferris (29) who didn't seem to have

any interest in complying with the permit that had been issued. Every month there were violations. The federal Water Pollution Control Act of 1972 required a federal permit. New York was delegated the responsibility to issue those. Biotech had a permit that was one of the first that were actually issued in the state, in 1977. It had effluent limitations that were really pretty basic — mostly BOD (30) and total suspended solids and things like that. And the Battenkill was a trout stream, so it had relatively stringent discharge limits. So for a whole lot of reasons like that, the case sort of floated to the top of a pile and got referred over to the New York State Attorney General's office.

"We sent some fish and wildlife guys out to the river, and they went upstream and downstream, and they documented that upstream things were healthy and abundant and the water quality was good, and directly downstream there was evidence of severe degradation, mostly from biological oxygen demand, which is the discharge of pollutants that take oxygen out of the water. The Attorney General's office tried to shut them down in 1979, but they failed because there was a battle of experts as to what the impacts were. But DEC continued to document the monthly discharge limit violations, and while I was at DEC we adopted

some regulations that basically said if you apply for a permit or a renewal, one of the grounds for denial is noncompliance with the permits.

"So in 1982, since these were five-year permits, they needed a new one, and that's where the state got them. The case is actually an interesting case because I think it's the first use of that section of law to deny a permit. And what that really meant was that Ferris and Biotech were out of business. Biotech appealed the case all the way up to the Court of Appeals and lost. They could have sold the plant to somebody else who had a different outlook on environmental compliance, but because the plant was such an old plant and so cob-jobbed and so marginal in so far as its economic utility was concerned, the plant was closed, I believe, in 1981 or 1982 and has been closed ever since.

"At the time, I never had any thought that I would be living on the Battenkill, downstream from that plant. Today, the empty, decaying structure at Biotech Mills stands for the proposition that if you ignore environmental requirements in New York and violate your permit month in and month out, when it comes time to renew the permit, it's not likely that you'll succeed."

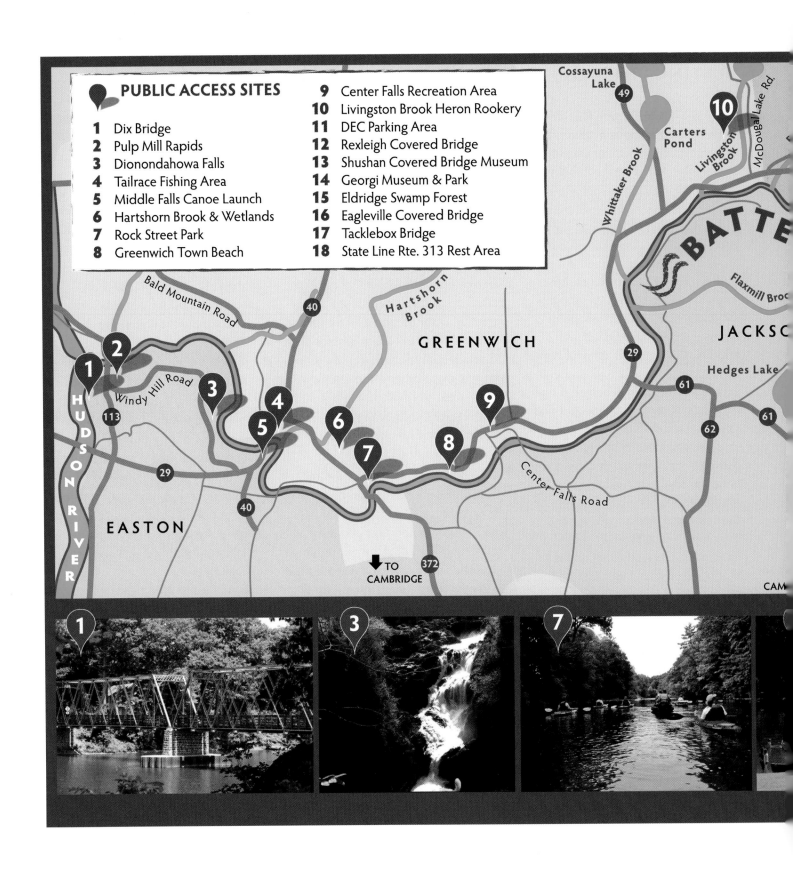

PUBLIC ACCESS SITES

1 Dix Bridge
2 Pulp Mill Rapids
3 Dionondahowa Falls
4 Tailrace Fishing Area
5 Middle Falls Canoe Launch
6 Hartshorn Brook & Wetlands
7 Rock Street Park
8 Greenwich Town Beach
9 Center Falls Recreation Area
10 Livingston Brook Heron Rookery
11 DEC Parking Area
12 Rexleigh Covered Bridge
13 Shushan Covered Bridge Museum
14 Georgi Museum & Park
15 Eldridge Swamp Forest
16 Eagleville Covered Bridge
17 Tacklebox Bridge
18 State Line Rte. 313 Rest Area

4. RECREATION

RECREATIONAL CONFLICT

"We saw something happen on the Battenkill that I think tells a pretty interesting story. We had a very successful canoe livery here for probably twelve years. They ran a great business. A lot of people enjoyed the river. And during that period, I fished a lot less because once a canoe passes through, the trout feeding activity will cease for a good thirty minutes. But we had an interesting thing happen then as a result of that period of conflict. A lot of other anglers like ourselves just stopped fishing the Battenkill and found other rivers to fall in love with. The Trout Unlimited chapter moved its energy and enthusiasm elsewhere, from the Battenkill to the Mettawee and the Poultney. And then the livery went out of business, and the anglers returned.

"But the overall message is that there is going to be increasing recreational conflict where one use interferes with or compromises another. I think as stewards, we need to step up to that challenge. We need to have those productive conversations to say, "How can this be a win-win?" Don't chase the protectors of the Battenkill off to some other place."

--"Perk" Perkins, CEO Orvis

A PLACE FOR RECREATION

Suzanne Piekarz operates Battenkill River Sports on a beautiful section of bottomland with almost half a mile of frontage on the river near Cambridge, New York. Her company rents canoes, kayaks, and tubes, and transports boaters to and from the river. She also maintains a scenic campground and a small Bed & Breakfast.(31)

EJC: Do you worry about people getting hurt on the river?

SP: I do nothing but worry. We have never had anyone hurt or killed. Of course they all sign a waiver. But we do a lot of consciousness-raising, which is not always appreciated. If someone comes in who is not capable of being in the river, I have to let them know.

EJC: So do they have to complete a questionnaire?

SP: No, but we do always ask if they have had experience canoeing or kayaking; and if they don't, then we offer them a tutorial, and we even ask them to go in the river from our beach, to do a short test run before they try a longer ride. That's all part of the package. There is no additional cost if someone needs instruction. They have to understand that there is a current. The big question for tubers is can you swim? They have to be able to swim to rent a tube. And we have safety measurements. Nobody can go in under 48 inches' height or 75 pounds' weight.

EJC: Do they get life jackets?

SP: Yes, everybody gets a life jacket. It's all part of the rental price. So yesterday was rough because I had a family show up, and I wouldn't put the child in the river because he was not tall enough, and they were upset with me. They wanted to put him in a tube, but we were able to compromise on renting them a canoe and putting him in it with his parents.

EJC: Did you grow up here?

SP: We permanently moved here from Westchester County when I was going into junior high. My father and mother and four brothers all moved up, and my parents bought this hundred acres from Isolene Marsh. Hers was the only family that had owned this land. Before the Marshes, it was the Abenaki (32). The Marshes bought the property way back when, and they divided it into perfectly square fields and cleared and de-stumped it. They had a very big barn here with 75 milking Holsteins by the late seventies, but it wasn't working out for them, and they decided to sell.

EJC: How did your family decide to come up here?

SP: My father was a hard worker, an electrician and a musician. He played the drums in a band. But my parents had a dream of owning a campground and a homestead where they could live off the land. At first, they looked down south, in Florida and the Carolinas. But he found this in a classified ad, and the price was very affordable. We got here, and my father signed the papers and moved in, but we had to sell all the cows because the farm help didn't want to work for him. They said they weren't going to work for a city slicker. But cows have to be milked, so there was no choice but to auction them off that night! But my father went ahead and laid electric and water lines and put up an attractive modern bath house, well up off the ground.

EJC: What are your plans for the future?

SP: My goal is to select the clientele so that we can enhance the beauty of the land and the experience of the natural history of the land for

those who really appreciate it. For example, for the last several years, we have hosted Overland, which is one of the oldest summer camps in New England. They come in with a little truck and counselors and prepare their own food and supervise the children. They get to camp in beautiful sites right on the waterfront. And I've contacted an on-line business that reaches out to youth groups all over the country. It's a website that anyone who is in education can use to find activities for their students, whether it be a Broadway play or a canoe trip on the Battenkill. I feel a very deep bond to this land, and I want to do everything I can to protect and nurture it.

Tubing on the "Kill"
near Jackson, NY
Claire Houston, photography

THE RACE OF '76

Jack Barber of Salem (33) recalled the Battenkill home-made raft race of 1976, the Bicentennial year, from the state line to the Eagleville bridge. "We received the trophy for finishing the furthest from our estimated time. It took us about four or five hours to make what should be a two-hour trip, if you behaved yourself. When we left here, we had all the equipment. We took boards; we took inner tubes; we took a spring; we took a mattress. It took us quite a while to assemble our boat. Mistake number one, we took two cases of beer with us that morning. So before we even left, that was gone. My brother Fritz was George Washington, and Charlie was Martha, and I don't know who I was. But once we got it going, we started down the river, and we were out of beer by then. So we would holler, and people would throw us some more. All of us knew people who lived along the river, so we would stop and visit and drink some more, stop and drink. We had sticks to guide the raft. The river that day was pretty deep. I would estimate that there were probably forty boats that went down through. At that time, it was really a big thing, and the banks were lined with spectators.

"One of the funny parts of it was that John Lundgren and his wife Judy were there, and John had a six-pack, and he met us half-way down. So we called out, 'John, give us a beer!' And he comes out, and what do we do but grab him and say, 'You're on the crew!' He said, 'You guys are crazy!' I replied, 'We could have told you that before we started.'"

Ken Sheffield added, "I think Fritz had diapers on, because the raft was called *The Birth of a Nation*. The gynecologist from Cambridge came down with his wife. They had two inner tubes tied together, and the name of their raft was *Tubes Tied*."

The race is still a vivid memory for Rob Southerland too.

"We put barn doors with 55-gallon drums underneath them that probably had had pesticides in them at one point in time, and we'd lash them together and put as much beer on top as we could. You could almost walk across the river [there were so many rafts]. And it was crazy. But things have gotten a lot better. The Battenkill Conservancy has done a real good job, and I don't sense the craziness that there used to be."

FISH TALES

Ken Sheffield (34) remembers his earliest fishing experiences.

"When I was young, about five years old, I liked to fish. My father liked to fish, but he didn't have a lot of time to take me fishing because he worked in the paper mill in Battenville, and he worked fifty-six hours a week, so he didn't have a lot of free time to go fishing, though when he did have free time, that's usually what he was doing. Anyway I was always driving my mother crazy to take me fishing because we lived right on the Battenkill, down in the back yard. But she was always busy and didn't have time to sit down by the river with me, and the water was kind of high too. So what she did was she took me down and tied a rope around my waist and tied the other end to a tree so that I couldn't fall in. And she told me, "If you untie that rope, that's it; you're not going to go fishing." So I didn't; I stayed there. I never fell in, and I got to go fishing anyway."

Instead, it was his mother who fell in.

*Boy Fishing with
River Chatter*
oil on canvas
Stephen Lack

"There used to be a dam in East Greenwich, which went out in the late 80's, and there used to be a good concentration of fish there, because the trout would swim upstream, and they would have to stop there. The old power plant had a spillway on the side of it, and the water was always flowing through there, so it had a lot of oxygen in it, and there were always a lot of trout in there. In fact on a sunny day when the sun was high, you could look down in there, and you could see all these trout. They were eighteen, twenty inches long, and I used to fly fish on the high wall, about ten feet up. If you caught a fish, you had to walk it down the wall and put your arm around a tree to get the rod and make it down to the river where you could land it.

"When the water went down a little in the spring, you could walk out on the concrete ends of the dam to fish. My mother was fishing on the end where there was a concrete apron with a pretty good slope to it, and she had hooked a good-sized trout and was trying to land it. She slipped and fell, rolled down the concrete and off the end. Anyway, she still held onto the fish, landed the fish, but she broke her collar bone and got two black eyes. Her picture showed up in *The Greenwich Journal*, with the headline, 'You Should Have Seen the Other Guy.'"

RECREATION

MELONS IN THE SAND PILE

The qualities that led to success at the Hand Melon Farm in Easton, New York, are no different today than they were in 1908 — experimentation, courage, and innovation.

In 1908, Aaron Hand retired from the downstate business world, moved to Greenwich and purchased a 175-acre dairy farm, a farm the neighbors jokingly referred to as "the county sand pile." After only a year, he passed away, leaving his 18-year-old son, Allen F. Hand, to run the family farm. (35)

In 1925, Allen decided to try a new exotic cash crop, muskmelons. He planted one acre of the melons in an alfalfa field. With some experimentation and adjustments to the planting process, he timed his harvest to coincide with the Saratoga racing season. By 1939, Allen was growing 18 acres of melons, had trademarked the name Hand Melon, and created the distinctive red and white logo you see today. The county sand pile had become a thriving business, and the farm became famous for its rare variety of melons known as the Saticoy.

Eventually, Allen's son, "AA", took over the thriving business. He shut down the dairy farm and focused on growing the fruit and vegetable operation. It was under AA's leadership that the Hand Melon Farm expanded from selling to distributors and retailing at their own farm stand on Route 29, to shipping "Mail-order melons" and starting a pick-your-own strawberry, blueberry, raspberry, tomato and pepper business.

Today, the Hand Melon Farm produces over 140 varieties of fruits, vegetables, herbs and ornamental fall gourds on 419 acres. They employ integrated pest management principles (36), crop rotation, composting and resting fields. AA's son John has conserved the land with the Agricultural Stewardship Association (ASA) and used the proceeds to improve the irrigation system and install solar panels and ensure that his family legacy would carry on.

With no debt, a state-of-the-art irrigation system, and no power bill for the next thirty years, John thinks his dad would approve. And you can see it all in action during the upcoming strawberry picking season in June.

Garden of Earthly Delights
Elizabeth Cockey, photography

5. AGRICULTURE

STEWARDS OF THE SOIL

Working farms shape the landscape and enhance the scenic beauty of the Battenkill watershed. The Agricultural Stewardship Association (ASA) was established in 1990 by farmers and conservationists to conserve farm land in New York's Washington and Rensselaer Counties. ASA acquires conservation easements from landowners to guarantee that farms will remain available for agricultural production. When a farmer gives up the right to subdivide and develop his property for residential purposes, the market value of the property decreases as a result; and ASA pays the farmer for that diminution of value. The funding comes from a combination of private donations and state and federal grants. Many landowners have also generously donated their easements to ASA.

Well tended farms shape the landscape and enhance the beauty of the Battenkill watershed.

"This is a voluntary program," said ASA's executive director, Teri Ptacek. "That's what is so beautiful about it. Our long term goal is fifty thousand acres conserved because we feel that that's what you need to maintain the critical mass required to support an entire community of farm-related businesses: the veterinarians, agricultural supply companies, seed and feed, and tractor dealerships. We also try to protect land that can be used for a variety of farming enterprises that will enable diversification." Some properties are consequently more worth conserving than others. ASA has created Priority Areas (using criteria such as soil quality, proximity to conserved land, and proximity to water resources) to help ASA focus its resources on better quality farmland. ASA has also set goals for conservation of farms within specific areas such as the Battenkill valley along Route 313 and White and Black Creeks in Salem. To date, the Association has placed 6% of Washington County and 5% of Rensselaer County under agricultural easements, for a total of almost 17,000 acres, about 4,500 of which are in the Battenkill watershed.

MANAGING A MICROCOSM

Camden Creek is a tributary of the Battenkill in Washington County, New York. It flows from north to south along the Vermont border near Shushan. Periodic flooding of the valley produces a rich soil. We found Flo Myrick mowing the first cut of hay on her farm in the Camden Valley. A graduate of SUNY in animal science and biology, she is passionate about horses and the land that supports them. After admiring her goats and some of the biggest and smallest horses we've ever seen, we walked with her to the creek. "Almost anywhere in this meadow," she said, "if you drill down for fence posts, you go down three feet, and you're at water level. And this is all gravel, at the end of the valley; so everything washes down to me. It's good and bad. I had no dandelions in my hayfield until the last flood. When you look at this soil, you'd think nothing could grow in gravel, but it's excellent, especially for grasses. When I bought this farm, it had been in corn for a long, long time. Corn is a heavy feeder. You don't get a lot out of it for the size of the plant. And it contributes more to erosion. I'm into horses and hay anyway, so I converted it to pasture and hayfields, which holds the soil better. You don't have to use chemicals like you do for corn, and you don't have to rely on GMO stuff."

She tries to avoid herbicides. "Another field down the road has a weed in it called bedstraw. (37) Bedstraw is almost impossible to get rid of when it takes over your field. So typically around here farmers want to kill it with Roundup and put it under. I'm on water table, and I have a well. I don't want to put Roundup on my field. I can't control what my neighbors do, but I can do my part. I have used commercial nitrogen fertilizer, but I haven't used any herbicides or pesticides. You have strength in diversity. Look at the variety of plants in this meadow. If you don't have a monoculture, you can have healthier soil. You don't need as much artificial help."

Pointing to a tree growing out of her silo, she talked about plans for the future. "I like to build things. This morning I drew a design to make the silo into an apartment so that I can do agri-tourism. The silo is twelve feet in diameter. You could add an observation deck/living/bedroom on the top, use the middle section for a bathroom/laundry room/storage, and do the kitchen with a porch on it at the bottom."

Flo realizes that we can't fix all of the world's environmental problems, but she decided early on that "I could manage a microcosm and make a really good place for people and animals and take care of that part of the world. You do the best you can as long as you can."

The Horses of Camden Valley
Elizabeth Cockey, photography

**"If you don't
have a monoculture,
you can have
healthier soil.
You don't need
as much artificial
help."**

A FAMILY FARM

Meg and Rob Southerland (38) run Gardenworks Farm, in the Black Creek Valley near the village of Salem, New York. We have been privileged to know the Southerlands for several years and featured a painting of their beautiful destination farm on the cover of *Drawn to the Land: The Romance of Farming.* Meg's grandfather McEachron purchased the farm in 1911. At that time, it was a dairy farm, one of many such small dairies in the region. He diversified to chicken farming, and his son, Meg's father, ultimately expanded the number of livestock to more than 200 cows and 50,000

chickens. Meg reminisced about the changes in agriculture since her childhood.

"Just riding the school bus on my way to school (we were five miles from Salem), there were probably ten small farms; and now it's all one big property [the McEachron farm] and close to the same number of tillable acres. So the valley is still under cultivation. There are more houses, but fortunately most of the land is still used for crops." The main crops are still hay and corn, though hay would have been more predominant fifty or sixty years ago. "Now they do haylage, (39) and baling hay is a thing of the past. There is a lot of corn silage. Managed wood lots are getting help in a tax break if we treat the woodland as a renewable resource and hire a forester to come in and assess what the tree maturity is, what should be cut, what should be saved. So everything is used. It's just one big farm. Black Creek [Farm] leases about a hundred acres from us. We have about three hundred, and they lease about a hundred tillable acres."

Rob commented that whereas the farmers used to be men, more women now own the farms along Black Creek. Meg recalled, "When I was growing up, you could help but not really lead and be in charge. It wasn't ladylike, and you'd have fun and be part of the scene. Maybe you were asked to feed the calves or something, but my mom and dad didn't want us to be in the barn with the hired men and learn the bad words."

"But today," said Rob, "Woody Hill, which is probably the largest dairy, Jim [Sheldon]'s daughter [Jenny] and her husband pretty much run it." Jim and Karen Sheldon have four daughters, and Jenny is the eldest, "and she definitely is a powerhouse."

Meg added, "Jessica Townsend was one of the first women that I remember milking cows, and she worked for this Woody Hill Farm and kind of broke through and showed how amazingly attentive women can be to a job like that.

"The other thing that's so different, when we were growing up, farms were expanding, and you needed more acreage if you increased your herd. And so the minute someone was going to retire — it wasn't as if anybody was going to move; you either died or retired — if there was nobody in the family to take over the farm, there would be a line of farmers to buy the property. And so this farm really was two farms, and then my dad inherited his grandfather's farm and then bought two other farms, and that ended up being 600 acres. And so all of the land was scooped up, and you'd buy a farmstead that might have 100 or 150 acres with only 60 good acres, but you bought everything. And you pastured young cattle in the less desirable fields and made it all useful. But all that's changed. Now smaller farms are being purchased by people who have a farm idea: make cheese, have a brewery, have alpacas; but it's different from dairies expanding."

Gardenworks Farm, Fall
as viewed from Route 30, Salem, NY
Peter Hanks, photography
Courtesy Gardenworks Farm

Today the lovely big white chicken barns at Gardenworks are used for storage of equipment. Boaters rent space for winter storage of their watercraft. Most of all, the Southerlands maintain the barns for their architectural beauty and historical significance. So few people are actively engaged in farming today that almost everything about Gardenworks has educational potential, and Rob makes a point of showing visitors how things used to be done. "It's really eye-opening to them," said Meg, "And in the barn Rob made

the plywood cutout cows; and that was to show people which end of the cow went into the stanchion. People would wonder. And they always talk about how hard farming looks, and you had to work on weekends and early and late; and things get done only if you make them happen."

"The mission too," added Rob, "and we feel strongly about this, is to really keep it a farm. We could go to Hand Melon and buy all the pumpkins, all the squash, and have them dropped off here, but we want people to know that we grow as much as possible from here." Another change in farming is that although local people may be doing the management jobs, Hispanics are the ones milking the cows morning, noon, and night. The foreign workers generally live apart from the locals, observing their own customs within their communities and wiring money home to their families. Asked how the foreign laborers are regarded by the citizens, Meg said, "I think there's a great acceptance because there's an understanding that local people won't work like many of these workers."

But further change may be on the horizon. Rob said, "A lot of farms of a certain size have gone to robotics, so they're no longer needing the milkers. And that will displace those folks for the big farms that can afford the machines." Then there's the automated corn planter that puts in 18 rows at a time. The farmer "can sit in it and press a few buttons and take a nap, and it'll have an alarm system that wakes him up when he's at the end of the field. And it will turn around automatically and line up so he doesn't overplant or miss a row.

But not that many people get that sophisticated here. The land's too hilly." There are other barriers to replacement of human labor. Small farms cannot afford robotic harvesters. Blueberries may be amenable to mechanized picking, but it would take a very refined robot to avoid squishing a raspberry.

For a time, farms were becoming larger and more specialized, but now in addition to large dairy operations, there are smaller farms that raise goats and make cheese, or grow fruits and vegetables and flowers. Several of the beautiful old farm houses, including the Southerlands', have become bed and breakfast attractions.

Asked whether she has noticed an increase in attention to water runoff management, Meg replied, "I think farms are very aware of rules and regulations, and there is great education through the Soil and Water office in Greenwich and the cooperative extension. When we hear Jim Sheldon talking, he's so aware of the number of feet he can be away from the water." Rob added, "The state has very strict regulations for the big dairies. There are strict requirements for the amount of manure that can be

"It wasn't as if anybody was going to move. You either died or retired."

spread, and that's why some of the people who farm have rented additional property, just so they have an area to spread the manure... I think the real thing is all the agrichemicals. Fifty years

ago, they weren't doing that. We couldn't lease the land to Don unless he was going to spray his corn and use ammonia to fertilize. That's just the standard practice that Monsanto and all the universities — Cornell and everybody — said do this for a good crop. So they're kind of locked in to doing that. Now there's a bunch of people up on Bunker Hill who are going organic. They won't have any corn; it's just going to be hay."

Sheep at Wedding Hill Farm (left)
Greenwich, NY
Barton Cockey, photography

Farm on the "Kill" (right)
oil on canvas
George Van Hook

ELIZABETH'S STORY: THE END OF AN ERA

My family has farmed along the Battenkill for over 250 years, as far back as the early 1700s when my 5-greats grandfather moved into the area from Connecticut. His son, Simon Stevens, Jr. fought in the Revolutionary war, survived and returned home to become a businessman and gentleman farmer. In 1837 he sold a parcel of property along the Battenkill, just east of the mill in Hard Scrabble (later renamed Center Falls) to Susan B. Anthony's father where Anthony built a home along the banks of the Battenkill.

Our farm spanned over 350 acres at one time and the Stevens' raised sheep, a successful endeavor because they had a robust market for lamb, which they sold during Easter time to the market in New York City. They prospered and their daughter Sarah married a man named Nathan Stewart who built a house in 1830 on the lower gentle slopes of the farm, just above the Battenkill. They called it Grand View because they could see all the way along the Battenkill and into Greenwich. Eventually their daughter Jane married Robert Stevens, great-great grandson of Simon. He continued to raise sheep on the property.

After my Grandfather Guy Barber came back from World War I, he married Robert and Jane's daughter, Fannie. Guy took over operations sometime in the early 1920s, selling off the sheep and purchasing cattle with the idea that dairy farming was a better market.

"My grandfather sold off the sheep and purchased cattle with the idea that dairy farming was a better market."

But in the early 1950s the dairy industry in Washington County had hit a downturn. Prices for milk were so low that my grandfather became alarmed, and decided to do something about it. At the time he was the head of New York State's Dairymen's association, and because of that, local farmers trusted him. I remember riding with him in his old Pontiac truck; it was filled with lots of milk cans in the back, all sloshing around as we drove to the milk processing plant where he said there was a meeting going on.

When we arrived there were a lot of other farmers there, all with cans of milk in the back of their trucks too. My grandfather picked me up and put me up on top of our milk cans, and then he climbed up. The other farmers gathered around and he started to talk to them, yelling to be heard above the crowd.

"Dump your milk," was basically what he instructed them to do.

"We won't sell any milk until we get a fair price!" he said.

And they dumped their milk, which created quite a mess, a white river that flowed all over the parking lot and eventually ran down into a drainage ditch by the processing plant. In the end, the farmers got what they considered a fair price for milk and my grandfather became the hero of the farming community.

"Dump your milk" was basically what he told them to do.

But disaster struck a year or so later in the summer of 1956. Lightning struck our beautiful yellow barn, which held a full loft of hay and one little Holstein calf named Jolly. I saw the lightning bolt hit, and then I saw my grandfather running across the lawn towards the barn, my father following. My father carried Jolly out of the barn, and my grandmother must have called the fire department, because it wasn't long before I heard sirens and then saw fire trucks pull into the driveway. My father told me later that they got water from the Battenkill to fight the fire, but despite heroic efforts of the fireman and local townspeople, the barn was lost. The ruins continued to smoke a week later, and to this very day I still remember the awful wet, ruinous, dank smell that emanated from charred piles of rafters, hay and farm equipment that was once the barn.

My grandfather, being who he was, did not let the loss of our barn deter him. I remember it was about a week later that he negotiated the purchase of the neighboring farm which was adjacent to our property, owned by the Faile family. He bought the place complete with barns and farming equipment, including a farm house. And so, in the spring of 1957 my father, mother, my sister, my brother and I moved out of the house we had shared with my grandparents next to the Battenkill, and into the new house "on the hill".

Grandfather Barber and my father Robert continued as dairy farmers until the early sixties when my grandfather decided they should get out of dairy farming altogether.

At that time the government and its agencies had just begun to implement new rules and regulations that eventually led to the demise of dairy farming for small farmers in Washington County.

And small dairy farms have not made a comeback yet.

Holsteins
oil on canvas
Leslie Peck

INDUSTRY

6. INDUSTRY

A SPORTING TRADITION

Orvis is the stuff of outdoor legend. Founded as a fishing tackle company in 1856 by Charles F. Orvis, the company thrived for over half a century but struggled during the Great Depression. Dudley ("Duckie") Corkran purchased it in 1939 and owned it until 1965, when Leigh H. Perkins bought the company and made it into a global fly fishing brand selling related lifestyle merchandise. Elizabeth and I met with CEO Leigh ("Perk") Perkins, Jr. and Vice Chairman Dave Perkins at the corporate headquarters in Arlington, Vermont. We asked to hear some good yarns.

Dave: One story about Dad illustrates how much time we spent on the Battenkill. There was a long period when Dad, Perk and I went out at night and fished the Battenkill. There's one of our employees, Nancy Perkins and her husband John, different family with the same last name. Five years ago, John was fishing in the Battenkill with his son, and somehow, down in the mud, they pulled out a wallet. They looked at the license to see whose wallet it was. It was my dad's wallet, and the license had expired some twenty years before. He was wet-wading and lost his wallet while fishing, and it stayed in the river that long! Imagine finding a wallet in mud. And the people who found it were Perkins and knew who Leigh Perkins was, and they returned the wallet!

Perk: I have a story to share with you that has to do with Dave and our deceased older brother Ralph. When my dad first bought the company in 1965, we were living in Cleveland, and we would come to Vermont and stay with Dad in the summer. He lived very much a bachelor's lifestyle here, because our mother had not yet moved. His idea of babysitting has always been basically to take us fishing or to put us in a fishing situation. So I remember a couple of summers where pretty much my whole summer was: Dad would drive to work about 7:30 in the morning and drop me off at the yellow house on the Battenkill with Ralph or Dave. We'd march across the fields with our fly rods, and we would fish our way up to the Union Street bridge by noon, at which point he would pick us up or we would walk up the hill to the office at Union Street.

The Famous Fishermen
Shushan postmaster Al Prindle and
fly-fishing legend Dr. Lew Oatman
Herb Eriksson, photography

We were in blue jeans or shorts and wet tennis shoes. We weren't deserving of waders back then. I was 12, Dave was 9, and Ralph was 14. And this is the great thing: we were muddy; we were wet; he would take us to lunch with him, because that's what a father should do right? And he knew he needed to feed us. So we would go to his business lunches and sit there eating in our wet clothes at the Colburn House, which was where North Shire Books is now. It was a nice but stuffy, old-school-type restaurant, where the waitresses wore uniforms. And then lunch would be over, and he'd drop us back down at the yellow house, and we'd fish our way back until the end of the day, when he would buy a steak — and usually just a steak—sometimes some corn on the cob or something like that; and we'd go *back* down to the river, and we'd fish. He'd cook the steak on the bank, and we'd get home at 10:30 at night. That was our upbringing for a couple of years. We learned a lot about fishing, nature, and how to stay alive on a river.

Dave: Even later, when Perk and I lived together on the farm, we'd come home from work, and there was generally a hatch (40) in that last hour every night.

Perk: When you're fishing in that last hour of light, it isn't unusual to catch a bat. You learn to make fewer casts after dark. I thought they called it the Battenkill because there were so many bats on it.

I remember coming back from one of those evenings of fishing. At that time, Dad had remarried, and our stepmother was a fabulous cook; so we would often finish our evening fishing and check in at their house, ostensibly to find out how the fishing was, but really to get a meal. So they generously would set the table, and it would be late at night. I remember one time we were eating and talking about fishing, and Dad, who has a wonderful sense of humor, was laughing and rocking back in his chair and started scratching his head. Suddenly he goes, "Ow, Ooh, Ow!"

And we ask, "What is it?" He says, "Oh, it's that fly!" He had caught himself in the scalp with his fly during the hatch and just snipped it off and totally forgot it was there!

Trout Fishing
oil on canvas
George Van Hook

" I think the view

is

secondary.

I like

the privacy."

BUILDING A BUSINESS

Al Brown is an entrepreneur in Greenwich, New York. His farm house nestles among hills so round and rolling that one almost loses all sense of horizontal and vertical. We asked him what appeals to him so much about the place that he calls home. What is the best part of living here?

"I think the view is secondary…I like the privacy. I like that vehicles aren't careening by at great rates of speed, although some people drive too fast on this road. I very much enjoy the isolation that happens, especially in winter."

Al got an early start in agriculture. He said, "I subscribed to Rodale's *Organic Gardening* (41) when I was nine and had an organic garden and sold produce to neighbors, along with eggs. I had chickens."

"So I schooled myself to be a builder, by trial and error. And this place was deserted when I bought it and had no power or water and probably could have been burned down by somebody but wasn't. And so I commenced to work on it and decided that I needed a job, and so I put an ad in the paper saying 'Slate rooves repaired' because nobody wanted to repair slate rooves. I ended up having a number of people working for me and doing a lot of building. Restoration was my favorite, but we built some houses and did some commercial work, all pretty much locally. At one point I decided, what if I got hurt? What would I do? So I go okay I'll be a real estate broker. So I go and take a test without reading anything, and of course I pass. Well, it's multiple choice. Two of the choices are stupid, so [even for the pure guesses] you have a 50 percent chance; so you have to get at least 75 percent. They don't tell you what you got.

"So I became a broker. And I found it to be a vehicle that fit with the construction because if people wanted land, I would sell it to them. In my experience, some people don't really care where they buy land if the price is right, if they can get their house on it, and it fits in their budget. There are a lot of people who have come here, especially from far away, who actually really appreciate the county and the land in the county and the Battenkill watershed way more than the locals, many of whom wish they could get out of here — or feel trapped. Maybe they don't wish they could be out of here but wish they could have better jobs. [The depressed economy] is getting worse, in my opinion."

Why, we asked, are similar farms so much more expensive just over the border in Vermont? His reply: "Wrong zip code." Asked to elaborate, he explained, "I think we have a skewed version of this because you can find rural places in Vermont that are like this where you can buy stuff for a similar price [farther north] or interior. And I don't know this for a fact, but this is my feeling. And we have, though not recently, driven up on the back roads, and you see the same kind of social conditions from the road. And so if there's a ski slope near, that influences the value of land and thus the value of farms."

Are property values in Washington County going up or down? "Real estate activity in this county, in terms of changes in price, is a function of that activity in the circle that surrounds this county at about 40 miles, meaning Albany, Troy, Glens Falls, Clifton Park, Manchester, and Bennington. And if that's stagnant, this remains stagnant; and typically we're less, so obviously we're not going to see a big blip if everything else is fixed or stagnant. And then there's the commutability issue, and more and more people are more and more dependent on things that aren't in this county. And so it's harder and harder to find your common consumer items in this county…If the Dow Jones goes to 3,000 and remains there and has decent growth, there'll be a whole lot of money in New York City, and people will want to retire and come up here and buy something — which is what drove the prices in the eighties and nineties."

Beautiful Water (right)
oil on canvas
Leslie Parke

THE DAM THAT NEVER WAS

Since the first settlers came to these parts, the Battenkill has attracted the attention of dam builders. The stream was seen as a resource to be harnessed or a wild beast to be tamed. Hardly anyone knows about the last and biggest idea about damming the river — a plan that fortunately never came to fruition. I am indebted to Jon Stevens for unearthing the following article (42) from the *Greenwich Journal*, July 4, 1923:

"A dam eighty-five feet high in the Battenkill valley about a mile above the village of Shushan is one of the details of the plans filed by the Hudson River Regulating District commission last week. There is no way of telling when such a project may be carried out, but the plans make it evident that the control of the Battenkill flow is counted an important feature of the state power development plans as formulated by engineers who have studied the subject.

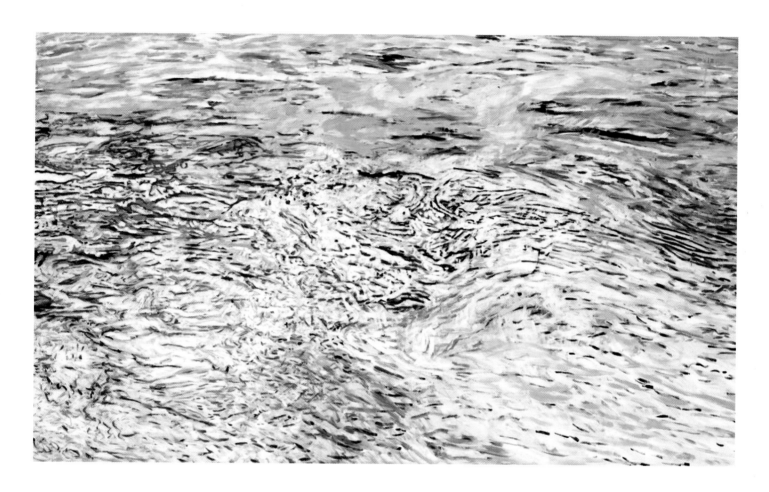

"When, and if, such a dam is built it will change the geography of Washington County to the extent of creating a lake bigger than any natural body of water now entirely within the county. Cossayuna, which now has the distinction of being the biggest lake in the county, not including of course, Lakes George and Champlain, which wash its borders, would be a good-sized pond beside the new Shushan reservoir, but not much more.

"The creation of Shushan Lake, according to the plans filed, would flood eight miles of public highway and two miles of the D. and H. railroad track. It would put the hamlet of East Salem under water and leave Anaquassacoke on the banks of a broad expanse of water. Going up stream along the Battenkill from Shushan, one travels almost due south for perhaps a mile and a half, then turns sharply to the north-east, from which general direction the stream flows from the Vermont border, a distance of several miles. The proposed reservoir would flood the stream far back toward the Vermont line. South from the big bend south of Shushan is a

Center Falls Mill (HV) (left)
oil on canvas (plein air)
James H. Kunstler

Pulp Mill Dam (right)
Photograph circa 1900
courtesy The Crandall Library
Folk Life Museum collection

broad plain between the White Creek hills and those in the town of Jackson. The maps indicate that a great expanse of this plain extending south toward Cambridge would be overflowed, and it is stated that the present water supply of the village of Cambridge would be flooded.

"The proposed storage reservoir is considered one of the most important ones in the whole district, as the Battenkill has a fall of 430 feet in the state of New York, and regulating the flow of the stream above the present power developments would add enormously to the value of these powers as well as develop an important power at the site of the new dam itself. The storage capacity of the proposed Shushan dam would be 3.4 billion cubic feet of water, if one can grasp the idea of what that sort of figures mean [sic]. The state estimates give the probable cost of this portion of the project as $1,600,000, or $470 per million cubic feet of storage."

"As people have become more aware of the side effects of dams, fish kill has become an issue."

THE GREAT FISH EXPERIMENT

Dan Shaw used to operate the two hydroelectric dams in Greenwich. He explained that the operating principle is simple enough: the river dumps water through the turbines and turns a generator.

"But the biggest issue you have is regulatory. As people have become more aware of the side effect of dams, fish kill has become an issue. They require you to make narrower spacing on your trash racks. You can't send trash through a turbine; it will jam it and plug it up or break it. Now if you take a stick three

Trout—The first Leap.

inches in diameter, those big blades will chew it up. So the spacing was set at three inches. But then they were concerned that fish could go through it; so they narrowed it down to an inch and a half. And at an inch and a half, what happens it that it plugs up with every piece there is. So cleaning the racks is the biggest part of any hydro operation. I did it twice a day. Some days you hardly had to do anything, but other days, especially when the leaves were shedding, it would plug it up. Then the electronics sense it and trip off the turbine so it shuts down, and you have to go over and clean it out and start it back up.

"But the real truth about the fish is that a healthy fish swims against the current. But here's the comical part: you have to do fish studies to prove you're right. How do you prove a healthy fish won't go down through the turbines? Well, here's what we had to do. It cost 75 thousand dollars. We had to put a fish bypass in to prove that a healthy fish would go through the bypass and not to the racks. They had to hire a team of wildlife biologist and engineers and then buy a whole bunch of fish, because that's what you've got to do. Now, these fish come out of a pond; they've never seen a current in their life. So the fish aren't dummies;

they aren't getting anywheres near anything. So you close the gate up on the intake so they can't get back up the river, and now you've got them in the canal. And you start up the hydros, and you open the gate so the water is flowing in, and you have to put a rack over the intake so they can't go up and out through the current. Now you've got your operation. You put a net on the turbine outflow (they call that the tail-race), so we had to have divers come and drill holes in the cement walls and put a net over it. And then we had the fish bypass; we had to put a net over that.

"The real truth about fish is that a healthy fish swims against the current."

"So then we ran it, and none of the fish went through, nowheres; stayed in there. So they go up there with electric prods, and they drive the fish down. And they get some that go through the turbines. They get some that go through the bypass. And the current is

whipping the nets and eats holes in the bottoms of them, and they find fish parts, fins that are stuck in the net because the current is so strong it's blowing them right through. So on the bypass, you see a lip or a tail, and you count it as a fish that knew enough to go through the bypass. Cost us 75 thousand dollars. And they wrote up a fifty-page report on how scientific this was. When we got done, the state fisheries said, 'Narrow your racks up to an inch and a half rather than three inches.' So we spent all that money and still did this. Not that I'm saying that in a bad way, but this is the bureaucratic part of operating a hydro."

INDUSTRY

THE PHANTOM OF THE KILL

Josh Levy is the owner of Phantom Laboratory, an almost invisible business off State Route 29 to the east of Greenwich, New York. The company makes simulated body parts used in testing and calibrating imaging equipment such as CAT and SPECT scanners. He spoke to us about the special qualities of the Battenkill valley. The greatest attraction of the region is that "it is a beautiful place to live. And if we realize, as Vermont has, that a great deal of our value is in our beauty, and it's worth preserving it, that's a huge step."

Josh is optimistic about the local economy. "I think that if you drive around at least southern Washington County, most of the residences look pretty good. I've lived in this area for about 35 years, and I've been full-time for about 27 years; and in that period of time, I think all of the communities look a lot better loved than they did way back. Now, that doesn't mean that there aren't a lot of people who can't find work or can't find good work. Like many areas of the country, the economics are changing. So we've lost businesses. We used to have catheter manufactures, and those are mainly gone now. They've gone of out of the country. Some went to Mexico and then

went overseas, to Asia or whatever. So there are losses like that, but there's also a number of businesses in the area which are really quite phenomenal, that people don't even notice when they drive by.

"We have Belt Dewatering Press, BDP, across from the fairgrounds. They do a lot of manufacturing of the equipment used to separate sludge from water in sewage treatment plants, and they've got some pretty cool machinery there. There's John Hedbring's company [the Fort Miller Company, which manufactures a wide variety of pre-cast concrete products for roads, bridges, and walls, as well as

"One of the neat things

about this area is

that the businesses

that are here tend

to be run

by members of

the community."

Looking into Vermont (left)
from the Braymer farm, Salem, NY
oil on canvas
Harry Orlyk

custom applications from canal locks to airport towers.] In Cambridge, there's Cambridge Valley Machining, which is a large machine shop, and they do neat custom work and have a very good reputation. In Argyle, we have Fronhofer Tool, which is expanding. They are putting up a new building behind the police barracks now. And their specialty is doing big stuff. In the machine world, if you want to turn a rod that's eight inches in diameter and twelve inches long, any machine shop that has a lathe can do that for you. But if you want to do something that's eight feet diameter and sixteen feet long, the only place you can find to do it in the area is Fronhofer Tool. So they do a lot of big things for mills, but they do a lot of specialized work, and recently they've even been making the tanks used by microbrewers to brew beer.

"One of the neat things about this area is that the businesses that are here tend to be run by members of the community, and it's not management that came in from somewhere to run the company in a factory owned by somebody somewhere else. Like anywhere,

technology is changing, and there are some businesses going down and others going up. It's great to romanticize the way things used to be, but I think in a way we have a lot more in this area than we ever did. Granted, the scale of farming has changed. For a farmer to raise a family and have fifty cows is not really an easy thing to do any more. On the other hand, we have clever people like Black Creek Farm with the creamery. They realized they didn't have any control, but now they process their own milk, and that's a huge success story.

"When we have people visit and have dinner at home, the greens and meat came from a local farmer, and the ice cream came from the creamery, and the cheese is from Gardenworks. In the suburbs of Chicago for example, go try to find anything locally grown. It all comes from somewhere else. Here, we know where our food comes from. So I think that although we can always do better, this is a really great place to live and work."

END NOTES

1. Fisher, Donald W., *The Rise and Fall of the Taconic Mountains*, Black Dome Press, NY, 2006.

2. Concerning the accomplishments of Ebenezer Emmons, http://ees2.geo.rpi.edu/history/emmons.html, retrieved 6/26/2016.

3. For a good summary of the career of this remarkable man, http://www.academia.edu/10940574/EBENEZER_EMMONS_AND_THE_SECOND_NORTH_CAROLINA_GEOLO GICAL_SURVEY_GEOLOGICAL_INVESTIGATIONS_AMIDST_A_TIME_OF_WAR, retrieved 6/26/2016.

4. *Ibid.*

5. McRae, Mary Ann, "A fishy name will stay the same," CNN web post, http://www.cnn.com/US/9609/06/fishy.name/, retrieved 6/5/2016.

6. Merwin, John, *The Battenkill*, Lyons and Burford,1993. John Henry Merwin (1946-2013) lived in Dorset, VT and was an angler, distinguished author, and veteran fishing editor for *Field and Stream* magazine. His book on the Battenkill is a must read. It favors Vermont as much as this volume slants toward New York.

7. Israel, Jonathan, *The Dutch Republic, Its Rise, Greatness, and Fall 1477-1806*, Clarendon Press, Oxford, 1995.

8. Swift, Esther Munroe, *Vermont Place Names*, Stephen Greene Press, Brattleboro, VT, 1977.

9. A web post from January 26, 2013 wrestles with the origin of the name and includes a highly unlikely suggestion, a bat cave near Mt. Aeolus near Dorset, VT. Such a cave would be too obscure to lend a name to the whole river, and the Dutch word for bat is vleermuis. Dolton, Patricia A., *Town of Greenwich Historian's Blog,* http://greenwichhistory.blogspot.com/2013/01/place-name-origin-battenkill.html, retrieved 6/27/2016.

10. Beauchamp, William M., *Aboriginal Place Names of New York*, New York State Educational Department, Albany, NY, 1907.

11. Cusick, David, *Sketches of Ancient History of the Six Nations*, Lewiston, NY, 1827.

12. Dan Shaw is the Easton, NY Town Supervisor. His property overlooks the Battenkilll near Clarks Mills in Easton, NY.

13. Bob Warren lives and makes music on the river just outside of the Village of Greenwich, NY. http://www.bobwarren.com.

14. Surreptitious nocturnal discharges of paper mill chemicals may be charming to the poetic imagination.

15. The famous fishermen: see page 14 for a photo of Al Prindle and Lew Oatman by Herb Eriksson.

16. Valla, Mike, *The Founding Flies, 43 American Masters, their Patterns and Influences*, Stackpole Books, 2013.

17. Harry Orlyk's work is widely exhibited. Current information is at http://www.harryorlyk.com.

34. Ken Sheffield is a retired school teacher in East Greenwich, NY, and an avid hunter and fisherman. Nobody is better at calling in turkeys.

35. This story about Hand Melon Farm was adapted with permission from the Agricultural Stewardship Association newsletter, Spring, 2015.

36. Integrated pest management (IPM) is a strategy for reducing the use of pesticides "through a combination of biological control, habitat manipulation, modification of cultural practices, and the use of resistant varieties." http://www2.ipm.ucanr.edu/WhatIsIPM/, retrieved 8/12/2016.

37. Smooth bedstraw, *Gallium mollugo*, is a perennial weed, distasteful to animals, with multiple stalks encircled by whorls of small leaves. Clusters of small, white to greenish flowers appear from late June through August.

38. Gardenworks Farm is a destination in itself. The website is http://gardenworksfarm.com/.

39. Haylage: By analogy to silage, hay is harvested before it is dry (40-60% moisture content, compared to 18% for normal hay bales) and sealed in plastic, so that anaerobic fermentation acidifies the plant material, preserving nutritional value and preventing spoilage.

40. Hatch: What fishermen call a "hatch" is actually a simultaneous emergence of flying insects from their aquatic nymph stage for a brief sexual fling as winged adults. Trout seem to have such a strong interest in the insect du jour that they will ignore artificial flies of the wrong variety.

41. The magazine's founder, healthy living expert J.I. Rodale (born Jerome Irving Cohen), dropped dead on the Dick Cavett show in 1971 immediately after predicting that his excellent health would see him through to the age of 100. He was 72 years old. The episode was not aired. Kelly, Keith J., "Rodale revamps 'Organic Gardening' to healthy lifestyle magazine", *New York Post,* August 23, 2014, http://nypost.com/2014/08/23/rodale-revamps-organic-gardening-to-healthy-lifestyle-magazine/, retrieved 7/10/2016.

42. "Would Make a Lake Just Above Shushan," *The Greenwich Journal,* July 4, 1923, p.1.

Additional Contributing Artists

George Van Hook resides in Cambridge, NY. His plein air landscape paintings are widely exhibited. He also produces remarkable figurative and still-life paintings. His website is www.georgevanhookfineartist.com.

Stephen Lack is an artist living in Washington County NY and exhibiting internationally. He is represented in many major collections. His works have appeared in the New Yorker Magazine, Glamour, GQ, and the NY Times. His films have debuted at the Whitney Museum and MOMA NY. His website is www.stephenlackart.com.

Clifford Oliver is a photographer living in Greenwich, NY. He is active in volunteer work and historical reenactments. His website is www.cliffordoliverphotography.com.

Leslie Parke lives in Washington County, NY near the Vermont border. She is renowned for her extremely realistic paintings and posts at www.facebook.com/LeslieParkeStudio.

Leslie Peck is an artist and illustrator living in Greenwich, NY. She has carried her expertise in portrait painting into the farm country with exquisite animal paintings. Her website is www.lpeck.com.

Seline Skoug is a photographer who has been interested in fly fishing since age 8. She is the founding Executive Director of Casting for Recovery (counseling breast cancer survivors and teaching them the art of fly fishing) and co-owner of a fly box company. Her website is www.selineskoug.com.

18. Bonnie Hoag describes her program in detail at http://www.dionondehowa.org/.

19. Charlie Tracy started driving trucks for his father at age 8 and is now happily retired from a sand, gravel, and concrete business that he founded in the vicinity of Greenwich, NY.

20. Jacob Houston has a unique style that has made him a rising star in the art world. His website is http://www.jacobhoustonart.com/.

21. Lehman, Don. "Eight years later, Jaliek Rainwalker's death still a mystery," *The* Post *Star*, October 30, 2015, http://poststar.com/news/local/eight-years-later-jaliek-rainwalker-s-disappearance-still-a-mystery/article_90047190-3cdc-5bab-a566-2b4a0d27d7f4.html, retrieved 9/3/2016.

22. Judy Flagg operated the shop Union Village Limited at 79 Main Street in Greenwich for many years, closing in 2016. Her husband Ken is an engineer employed by the State of New York.

23. James Howard Kunstler is the author of a series of novels about life in a small main-street town (loosely based on Greenwich, NY) after the political and economic collapse of the entire country: World Made by Hand, The Witch of Hebron, History of the Future, The Harrows of Spring. The Battenkill features in all of them. He is also an artist and violinist. More about his books, as well as his commentary on peak oil, urban planning, and the parlous state of the world, may be found at http://www.kunstler.com.

24. Karas, Nick, *Brook Trout,* Skyhorse Publishing, New York, 1997.

25. Joshua Ness and the knotweed, http://www.skidmore.edu/news/2007/345.php, retrieved 5/6/2016.

26. Smith Ann Wright is a native of Greenwich, NY, and one of Elizabeth's childhood friends. She used to work as an editor for the Greenwich Journal and has kindly helped with the editing of this book.

27. Howard Romack is an Adjunct Researcher at the Biological Survey at the New York State Museum. He continues to inspire local youngsters with his dramatic presentations of live snakes, turtles, aquatic invertebrates, and more.

28. McCabe, T.L. and Wagner, D.L., "The biology of sthenopis auratus," *ENVIRON. ENTOMOL.,* vol. 19, no.4, August, 1990, 916-925. (The moth's name has since been changed to *Sthenopis pretiosus.*)

29. Marvin C. Ferris, President of Biotech Mills, was born on April 1, 1917 to Ukrainian immigrants named Clara and Samuel Fiddleman and died June 16, 2012 at his home in Greenwich, NY. http://www.legacy.com/obituaries/saratogian/obituary.aspx?pid=158110318, retrieved 7/19/2016.

30. BOD: Biochemical oxygen demand. Some pollutants reduce oxygen levels in the water.

31. Battenkill River Sports is one of two outfitters operating on the river. The respective websites are: battenkillriversports.com and battenkillvalleyoutdoors.com.

32. The Abenaki people were a group of Algonquian-speaking tribes of northern New England and southern Canada. They allied themselves with the French during the Anglo-French wars. Their descendants are still living in the same regions. Four Abenaki bands finally received official recognition by the State of Vermont in 2012. http://vtdigger.org/2012/05/08/vermont-governor-legislature-formally-recognizes-abenaki-bands/, retrieved 7/29/2016.

33. Jack Barber (November 2, 1932 - October 30, 2016) was a beloved school teacher and coach in Salem, NY.